If You Can

Here's How To Get I

by **James Breckenridge Jones**

Edited and with Forward by **Dr. Robert C. Worstell**

First published in the 1957, no renewal found on record.

This edition copyright © 2014 Midwest Journal Press. All Rights Reserved.

Visit Midwest Journal Press for more materials and related books.

http://onlinesecretsreview.onlinemillionaireplan.com/p/books-courses-and-material.html

Table of Contents

Forward...1
Introduction..4
1 – If You Can Count to Four..6
2 - The Secret of Genuine Success..22
3 - Awareness Is Power!..30
4 - Choosing Your Goal...38
5 - You Can Have Self-Confidence..46
6 - Money: What It Is, And How to Have Plenty of It.............54
7 - How To Make Success Automatic.....................................63
8 - How To Obtain The Missing Ingredients Necessary For Your Success..71
9 - The Power Which Makes All Desires Obtainable..............79
10 - The Power of your Imagination.......................................87
11 - How To Obtain An Increase In Income...........................93
12 - The Power of your Emotions...99
13 - How To Get Started On Your Dream.............................104
14 - The Four Greatest Values In Life...................................112
15 - How To Get A Feeling...116
16 - The Power of the Law of Repetition..............................121
17 - Some Usual and Unusual Examples of The Count to Four Technique..126
18 - Questions and Answers...142
Bonus – The Millionaire Maker Lecture: "How To Get Everything You Want Out Of Life"......................................157
Supplement: Count to Four Technique Study Guide............170
Addendum...193
Resources..194

If You Can Count to Four - 1

Forward

The story of this book is fantastic. It has been "lost" for so many years, yet the lives it affected during that time are innumerable.

It's probably affected yours as well – in ways you haven't known.

You've heard of most if not all of these "greats" of the self-help, inspirational, and motivational fields:

Tony Robbins, Mark Victor Hansen, Jack Canfield, Brian Tracy, T. Harv Eker, Chris Widener, Mark R. Hughes, Les Brown

All these were influenced by **Jim Rohn**.

Rohn, along with *Zig Ziglar, Mary Kay Ash, and Bill Bailey* were directly influenced by

Earl Shoaff – who was known as the Millionaire Maker.

Shoaff was in turn influenced by **Dr. J. B. Jones** – who influenced countless others with his book and speeches.

It is there where we find yet another Source of Success – one of it's true evangelists – who made other evangelists, who in turn made evangelists, and so on. Like the successful trainer who successfully trains successful trainers to train.

Yes, that seems a mouthful.

Dr. Jones became a millionaire many times over, trained Shoaff (the "Millonaire Maker") who in turn trained other training-millionaires who continue to help others manifest their own abundance.

While in this book, Jones describes how he worked his way up from his poverty-stricken beginnings, both Shoaff and Rohn were also basically flat broke when they discovered Jones' teachings – and within 4 years or so of learning, internalizing, and applying the principles this book contains, each became multi-millionaires – as well as those who took up the challenge.

Did you then strike a rich vein for yourself by finding this book?

Let's not stop there - the mystery continues: who did Dr. Jones learn his secrets from?

If You Can Count to Four - 2

In this one and only book Jones was ever known to write, he gives the mentors he had studied under:

Robert Collier, Thomas Troward, Napoleon Hill, Louis Grafe, Joseph Murphy, Neville Goddard, Wallace Wattles

In short, Dr. Jones internalized some of the greatest minds of our age – writers who each themselves came up with very potent prescriptions for the world's ills.

What can we then learn from this single lost book after all this time?

Probably the core principles and laws which govern true wealth and abundant thinking which have been true since before recorded history.

But you are going to have to test this out for yourself.

There is no one forcing you to do it. The fact that Jim Rohn was completely broke when he met Shoaff at a lecture, and Shoaff was destitute when he met Dr. Jones, and these all became rich and helped their followers become millionaires and multi-millionaires – these facts alone show the vital workability of this book.

This book was published in 1957 and even today, people who have uncovered it have found it to be life-changing.

This modern edition is based on the most powerful first edition, which urban legend has was pulled from circulation and all copies destroyed – so subsequent versions could be edited to be "less disruptive" to the reader's life.

- - - -

It's been my honor to bring this into our modern digital age – and republish it in hardcopy as well, for everyone to find.

If you choose to take this opportunity, you can learn from it and the other books in this series.

You can become millionaire with what's covered here – or make more millions or even billions.

Meanwhile, you can achieve true self-confidence, self-esteem, attain your dreams – and know all the tools so you can continue to do this the rest of your life in any way you want.

Of course, this is only if you decide to take this seriously and really apply it to your life.

If You Can Count to Four - 3

And you are going to have to test everything and accept nothing at face value – including especially what I've said so far.

For your life is just that – your life. *For better or worse, your life is just and only what you make of it and with it.*

So let me get out of your way...

Good Hunting – and Good Luck.

Dr. Robert C. Worstell
August 2014

Introduction

I am not in the book business. A book, to me, is one way of sharing an idea. I believe that when one feels strongly that he has an idea which would be a great value to others, it is his obligation to share it with as many others as possible. I have such an idea. I have been sharing it through other means, for some time, and many thousands of people all over the world have led me to believe that they have received much benefit by having learned about the idea and appropriating it. So, here is a book that is written for the express purpose of sharing an idea that will make available the answer to the problem of happiness, health and prosperity.

Yes, anyone who will, in the spirit of humility and sincere desire, study and learn how to use the ideas contained in this book, can enjoy a full measure of happiness, health and prosperity according to his individuality.

There is an infinite abundance in this universe. Not only is there an infinite abundance of happiness, faith, love, courage, joy, humility, wisdom, generosity, peace, gentleness, meekness, patience, kindness, and all such qualities one could ever desire to express habitually, but *there is an infinite abundance of every material thing that one could ever desire to have in order to express his individuality.*

The reason that so many people do not have the above in abundance is not because there is any shortage, it is simply because they are not aware of how to push the right button of appropriation. All things that one desires are available to one who understands the "Laws of Appropriation."

In other words, there is a simple set of rules by which all things are obtained, which anyone who really wants to learn them can learn and then be whatever he wants to be and have whatever he wants to have.

Yes, it is just that simple, and I want to share this idea with every person in the whole world, who is not already enjoying the full measure of life according to his individuality. I will speak mostly from experience, as I too, was poor, unhappy, and sick before I learned these simple rules. But now I am happy, healthy and more prosperous than I had ever dared dream before in my life.

If You Can Count to Four - 5

Yes, this book tells anyone how to make his dreams come true. I challenge you to turn your back on all suggestions to the contrary and to get a new lease on life and began now to assume the captaincy of your own soul and design the type of person you really want to be, and design the things you really want to have and accept them and soon they all will become a reality.

If you will learn the ideas contained in this book and use it, I guarantee that you will realize your most cherished dreams.

1 – *If You Can Count to Four*

If you can count to four, you can learn a simple set of rules which will unlock the treasures of the universe in all its dimensions.

Millions of people have been taught to believe that the rules of success are indeed so very difficult and complicated that surely they could never learn them.

The average person is perfectly willing to accept the fact that several hundred families in most any community are successful. They, at the same time, know that there are hundreds of communities in our own country and, of course, and all the other countries too.

If they would stop and think for a moment, they would also know that when you add up the hundreds in each community, and then multiply by the thousands of communities all over the world, that it would add up to hundreds of thousands of people who are very successful.

For example, not long ago it was my pleasure to visit Mexico City. I was surprised to learn that there are approximately 10,000 millionaires in Mexico City. We hear of the millions of extremely poor people in the country of Mexico. But, at the same time, there are 10,000 millionaires in just one city in Mexico. How could there be that many rich people and millions of poor people unless there is a basic system of rules that 10,000 of them are using and the millions are not using? I too, wondered about these perplexing problems for many years.

I was born into a family of 14 children down in the hills of Tennessee and the first 18 years of my life I was what was considered a poor boy. I observed hundreds of families who obviously were not poor. They had poise, culture, a feeling of well-being, self-confidence, a measure of health, and they had plenty of money to express life abundantly. I wondered why my wonderful parents did not have those things in abundance too. I was stirred to investigate and find out, if possible, the answer to this problem.

I found out that anyone can be genuinely successful if he will learn the exact same "rules" that the successful people learned and use them.

If You Can Count to Four - 7

To be genuinely successful, to me, is to enjoy a large measure of happiness, health and prosperity. It is a balanced type of life; Harmonious living with good physical health and also plenty of money.

So, it was my privilege to start out as a poor, unhappy person and to make the same observations that the millions are now making. It was my privilege to learn these basic rules and to take them out into the hard-boiled business world and to challenge every one of them. *And to discover, beyond any shadow of a doubt, that there not only is a system of rules, but that anyone, not just a few, can learn them and use them and become just as successful as he wants to be.*

The title of this book, "If You Can Count to Four" is designed to tell you that regardless of your background, your lack of education, your lack of knowing anyone who is supposed to be important, your lack of funds, or any other seeming lack, you can still be what you want to be and have what you want to have.

Yes, you can start right now without funds, without education, without friends or influence, without an idea, without anything but a sincere desire to be somebody expressing life, and you can be that person you have secretly always wanted to be, and you can have all the money you want to express yourself within every field of your own choosing.

Are you ready to put The Count to Four technique into action? I am sure that you are. I know that you are because I know that you have many desires which you have never realized.

It has been said that 98 people out of every 100 have never decided just exactly what they want to be in life. That is, they have never come to any decision regarding a "life's goal" like Henry Ford, Thomas Edison or Andrew Carnegie. But here is the most important thing as far as I am concerned. It is understood that 98 out of every hundred haven't made that big decision, but I happen to know, and you do too, that you and I and every other person living at this moment has some desire, right at this moment, that we want to realize as soon as possible.

Ask yourself the question, "What do I want to be next?" "What do I want to attain next?" List all the things you want to be next and all the things you want to have next. Let's not worry too

If You Can Count to Four - 8

much about what we want next year or five years from now or 20 years from now, at this point. If you have just one little desire right now that you wish fulfilled and you don't know exactly how to go about it, then you are ready to learn how to "Count to Four".

Let's begin by looking at **Phase One** which is to i*dentify what you want*.

Write it down.

Define it.

Describe it.

There are several ways of helping your subconscious mind to become deeply impressed with exactly what you want. For example, you can cut pictures out of magazines and paste them in a scrapbook. If you can draw well, or if you know a friend who is an artist, you can create drawings or pictures of your idea of what you want.

By going through this simple mental process, your subconscious mind is impressed with exactly what you want. I want to point out, right at this point, that what I am asking you to do does not cost you one red penny. I merely want you to do it so that we can cause your mind to go through certain "thoughts."

You see your thoughts as size and color and texture. One of the reasons a person is living a small, limited type of life now is that he is in the habit of thinking small, limited thoughts. So, for Phase One, *let's not ask the price*.

Let's just identify what we really want. It can be any size and color and texture and design. At this point, all we are concerned with is "a mental process" which does not cost a cent. So, do what I am asking you to do, because if you will, I guarantee you that you will realize your desire in every case.

So, with the humility of a little child, get yourself a notebook and write down everything that you want to be next and everything that you want to have next. First of all, just write them down in your own words so that you can read them and they will cause you to know what you want next.

Then, after you have written these things down, start cutting out the pictures which represent what you want and paste them

If You Can Count to Four - 9

in the notebook. For example, I have done this in regard to automobiles, and I have known many of my students to do the same. I decide that I want a certain automobile, then I write it down in my notebook. I go down to the dealer and obtain as many color pictures as possible and then I paste one of them in my notebook, on the wall by my bed, in the bathroom by the mirror and in my desk, so that every time I open the drawer I see the picture of what I want.

By doing all these things I accomplish the purpose of the ONE phase of of the formula of success. *I developed a keen, clear, distinct mental picture of exactly what I want.* The subconscious will help us obtain exactly what we want or if we give it a hazy, unclear, smeared concept or mental picture, it will help us obtain that.

Which would you rather have, just exactly what you want or a smeared, unclear approximation of what you want? I can tell you from hundreds of experiences that this works right down to a "T."

I might say here, that *of the thousands of successful people whom I have studied, every one of them had either consciously or unconsciously developed the ability to think distinctly and clearly, and to define and identify the things which they wanted.*

The millions of people who do not have the things they want, at the same time, have not developed their ability to think clearly. Yes, they had the same basic ability to learn to think distinctly as anybody, but they did not realize that it was important or that it had anything to do with him getting what they wanted, so they just continued to think in a blurred, indistinct manner.

When I found this out in my research I was deeply impressed and immediately started trying to think more clearly. I began to identify exactly what I wanted to be and have. I noticed right away, a change in my life. I had more of a feeling of harmony and peace as soon as I took charge of my thoughts and started to define distinctly what I wanted to be and have. Also, my financial situation began to get better and better.

Most of you will say at this point, "Well, I can certainly accomplish Phase One." As long as it doesn't cost anything, what have I got to lose? You say to yourself, "If there is just one remote possibility that this will work, even though I do not

If You Can Count to Four - 10

quite understand just how it works, I am certainly going to get started right away and obtain a nice notebook, and write down my secret dreams of what I have always wanted to be and I am making a complete list of everything I want of a material nature.

"Since all he is asking me to do at this point, is to go through the mental activity, the least I can do is cooperate with him, as he promises me that I can be what I want to be and that I can have what I want to have. I am approaching this with just simple childlike faith as he has tested in his own life and many thousands of others and it has never failed.

"I don't have to understand just how it works, anymore than I have to understand the way my television set works in order to enjoy it fully; or anymore than I have to be an electrician in order to enjoy all the fine things which I enjoy through electricity. I must assume that there are 'laws' about which Dr. Jones is familiar, and he is sharing with me a simple little, one, two, three, four routine, which, if I follow, I can enjoy the full benefit of as though I understood it fully.

"I know that even little child can just turn on a light switch and not know anything about how it works, and all the lights will burn just as well for the child as if an expert electrician had turned on the light switch."

I must say just one more thing before I take you into the next phase which is Phase Two. I know that most of you will believe in this enough to try it. I congratulate you, because when you try it, you will find that it works.

And, of course, you will become what you want to be and you will have what you want to have. But there will be a few who think that they are so smart, that they will say, "Ah, that Jones guy is crazy." I would like to challenge you, if you should fall into this type.

Go ahead and prove me wrong. You can never honestly say that it won't work unless you try it and see whether it works or not. Go ahead, try it and prove me wrong. I have a pleasant surprise for you. You will end up being what you want to be in having what you want to have.

Now, let's move to Phase Two.

If You Can Count to Four - 11

Phase Two is also just a mental exercise, and it doesn't cost you one red penny. Phase Two is as follows: *"Pretend" that you already are what you want to be, and that you already have what you want to have.*

Ask yourself, "How would I feel if I were already the person I want to be? If I already had the things that I have written down on my Phase One list, how would I feel? What would I do? Where would I be right now?" In other words, assume the fulfilled dream.

Assume the feeling of the dream fulfilled. When a farmer plants a field of corn, he cultivates it, rains fall on it and the sun shines on it and it grows and grows until one day it is ready for the harvest. You see, Phase One of this formula is like planting the seed. Phase Two is like watering, cultivating and warming the soil by the sun shining on it. When you "pretend" that you are the person you want to be, you go through special mental activities or mental exercises which are like plowing the corn, or cultivating it.

When you assume the warm, deep emotional feeling of the person you want to be, it is like the warm sunshine shining on the growing corn. I can tell you many details of what actually takes place inside you and what happens in the whole universe, when you "pretend" but believe me, I know that if you will do it in simple childlike faith your dreams will come true. Is that fair enough at this point?

Later on, for those of you who are interested, I will be happy to go into the deeper aspects of the laws involved.

Someone will ask, "How do I comfortably go through these mental exercises of pretending that I am a certain person in my dreams?"

One of the best ways that I have ever used is as follows:

1. I first assume that I have already attained my desire.

2. Then I ask myself what event would normally take place after I had attained my desire but would never take place other than if I had attained my desire.

3. Then I make arrangements to live that event as though I had already attained my desire.

If You Can Count to Four - 12

For example, I went on the air on my first television program on June 19, 1955. I had my desire to be on television written down for several months before June, 1955. So, in March, 1955, I arranged an occasion to dramatize an event which would normally only take place after my first appearance on television. I arranged to have a debut party at my house, and the time was, as we pretend, the evening after I had debuted on TV that afternoon.

Each guest was invited and given a script, which told him exactly what to say at the party. So each guest arrived with great joy and enthusiasm congratulating me on having done a fine job that afternoon on my first telecast. All evening, our discussions were regarding how happy we all were that the program had been launched so well in the great good that would be done by the principles of genuine success being taken to so many hundreds of thousands of people, etc.

We pretend that we were celebrating the start of a television program in March, but the actual program did not start until June or about three months later. But we all assumed the mental attitude, the excited feeling, the tones of reality, of having already started the program. I happen to know that by doing this very thing it played a very important part in bringing my dream into fulfillment so soon.

You don't have to do anything great in order to use this one, two, three, four technique.

Let's suppose that your little girl wants a new tricycle. One day you see her riding an old broom around in the backyard. You ask her what she is doing and she says, "I'm riding my new red tricycle." She is using the same technique. She, first of all, did Phase One, which is to decide that she wanted a new red tricycle; then she was doing Phase Two by riding the broom and pretending that it was already her actual new red tricycle. It's just that simple. It doesn't cost a penny so far, and it's just a mental activity which you go through like a little child.

Let's suppose that you want to be a person who has great poise so that you can meet all life situations without fear or feeling of nervousness. You would even like to be able to stand up and speak before groups with poison comfort. Then, if that is what you want, you have your Phase One part already.

If You Can Count to Four - 13

What about Phase Two? You would do several things. Every time you attend a group meeting in the person of poise gets up and gives a really good speech, you see yourself as being the person giving that speech. Get that feeling of giving that speech by pretending that you are the person giving it. Also, give a party and coach your guests and celebrate your having given a great speech the day before. Also, line up some chairs in your living room, and one day when no one is there but you, assume that all those chairs are full of people.

Stand up and talk to them as long as you can think of anything to say. It doesn't matter at this point, just keep standing there and keep talking about anything whatsoever, and after a while you will get a feeling of comfort and you will then begin to control your thoughts. Then, after awhile, you will find yourself taking advantage of every opportunity of accepting appointments to speak before groups and you will one day find that you are a person of poise and confidence.

It doesn't matter whether you want to be the President of the United States, and Ambassador to a foreign country, a Congressman, a Senator, a movie star, a great singer, a great industrialist, a great attorney, a great salesman, a great farmer, a great housewife and mother, a great secretary, or a great whittler, you can become anything you want to be, big or little, by applying this one, two, three, four technique.

Can you fulfill Phase Two? Sure you can. All you need is the desire and humility of a little child.

But Phase Three is very important.

Phase Three is, *"That ability within you to say, Yes and No."*

Many people have not learned that it is their individual prerogative to evaluate any life situation or event or proposition and then down deep inside say, "Yes" if they believe it should be yes, and to say "No" if it should be no. I am not advising you whether, in certain circumstances, you should say "yes" or "no", but in order to emphasize this point, I would like to say that you have the power, and the right, and the ability, if you choose, to use it; and the God of Heaven gave you that power, right, and ability to use it.

Yes, you have within you the power, the right and the ability to look your father and mother right in the face and say "yes" or "no." You can look your minister right in the face and say "yes"

If You Can Count to Four - 14

or "no." You can look your husband, or your wife, right in the face and say "yes" or "no." You can look your friend, or your so-called enemy in the face and say "yes" or "no." Yes, you can look even God in the face and say "yes" or "no", because he gave you "dominion" and that means that you can say "yes" or "no" to every source of suggestion, even your God, and face the possibility of enjoying the results of having made the right decision, or of suffering from having made the wrong decision.

But the point I am making is that you were given the right, the power, and the intelligence, and the ability to learn to say, "yes" or "no."

Now, you have followed the suggestions made in Phase One and Phase Two very closely. But, one day you will happen to mention what you are doing, to a friend, your husband or your wife, your mother or father, your minister, and one or more of them immediately begins to make fun of you or discourage you. They tell you, "You mean that you fell for that!"; "Don't be silly"; "I don't believe that stuff, and I think that you are nuts"; or some sort of discouragement.

Well, Phase Three of this technique is "down deep inside you." Pay no attention to them whatsoever, but keep your thoughts on Phase One and Phase Two. Keep identifying your desires, and keep "living in the feeling of having already attained them." *Yes, you can control your attention units. You can learn to say "no" to anything which will hinder the fulfillment of your dreams.* You are the master of your fate, the captain of your soul!

Again, let me stress that so far it doesn't cost anything. When I lecture on the subject around the country I consistently have people ask me, "How much does it cost me to quit being what I am now and become what I want to be? How much does it cost me to get the things I want now?"

Well, I tell them that I had discovered and have proved a simple little technique that really works every time. It is called the "IF YOU CAN COUNT TO FOUR TECHNIQUE" Phase One doesn't cost one cent. Phase Two doesn't cost a cent. And Phase Three doesn't cost a cent either. And now, let me tell you that Phase Four doesn't cost a cent either. Is that fair enough?

Phase Four is the *HOW!*

If You Can Count to Four - 15

How do you get from here and now, to there, and what you want to be, and have what you want to have and not cost you anything?

Well, I am going to give you the answer in several ways so that you will be sure to trust it. First, let me say, that I am aware of certain facts, laws, rules, powers which are all natural, and which, if you will do certain things with the simple faith of a child, will all work for you and bring your dreams all fulfilled to you.

How many of you have ever had an idea come to you for "out of the blue?" All of you have, I am absolutely sure. Well, how many of you know just where the "blue" is located? I don't exactly know where it is located myself, but I know the name we give it.

The "blue" is your subconscious mind.

Now, your subconscious mind is like the "soil" into which the farmer plants seeds. The farmer plants for example, wheat. What grain does he expect to one day harvest? "Wheat, of course" you say. May I ask you "How does the farmer take one bushel of wheat, plant it in good soil and a few months later harvest, say 40 bushels? Where does the extra 39 bushels come from?" "Oh," you say, "Nature did it."

Well, the farmer has learned by experience that there is something, some power which he calls nature and that if he plants good seed in good soil in good season he can depend on this power in some manner or means which he does not completely understand to take his one bushel of wheat and increase it to 40 bushels.

At the same time, he knows this power does not steal this extra 39 bushels from the neighbor's granary. This power, in some fashion not fully understood takes just one bushel of seed, about an acre of soil, and about three or four months time.

The faith of the farmer, the warmth of the sun, the moisture of the rain, and other invisible elements, are combined and out of what appears to be "Nothingness" produces 40 new bushels of wheat. The farmer is pleased with the whole affair and his neighbor is not angry with him.

- Well, Phase One is the seed.

If You Can Count to Four - 16

- Phase Two is the watering, cultivating, sunshine and faith.
- Phase Three is keeping the weeds out and not letting the enemy destroy your seed which has been well planted and is being cultivated until the harvest.
- Phase Four is the Subconscious Mind, which has the same quality in the field of LIFE as the soil has for the farmer.

In this way, the same as the soil takes one bushel of wheat and gives you forty fresh, new bushels of wheat, the subconscious takes one good idea, and through laws only known to itself, makes it into your dream fulfilled.

But you ask, "Just how are some of the ways that this all develops, or comes about in my daily life?"

I am glad to give you several examples.

Remember that you have done what it says to do in Phase One. Also, Phase Two and Phase Three. Now, there is a "period of time" that it takes the seed to germinate and the harvest to arrive in the form of your dream fulfilled. This all takes place quite naturally from day to day in your life. But each day you will have ideas come into your mind and you will do what these ideas suggest as they have to do with the progress toward the attainment of your desires.

For example, suppose that you want to enjoy the standard of living which requires an income of one thousand dollars per month. But right now, your income is only three hundred seventy-five dollars per month.

- Phase One, you identify your desire of an income of one thousand dollars per month.
- Phase Two, you pretend and feel as you think you would feel if you already had an income of a thousand per month.
- Phase Three, you would insist on maintaining that feeling regardless of any suggestion which would disagree with you.
- Phase Four, you would listen for an idea from your subconscious mind which will help you to actually earn

If You Can Count to Four - 17

and receive the thousand per month. One day, you ask a friend of yours, "How many ways are there in the world, which pay at least a thousand per month income?"

He tells you of over one hundred ways that pay at least that much. Your Subconscious Mind begins to function in a manner that it never has before. It begins to add things up for you. It tells you in the form of ideas, out of the "blue" and in the form of feelings and urges that you should begin to study in a certain field, perhaps attend a series of lectures, or read certain books, or attain the necessary training to qualify for this new method which will permit you to earn and receive at least a thousand dollars per month. Of course, you not only listen to the subconscious, you do what it tells you to do.

You then, one day, find yourself in a new position that you enjoy very much and you are happier than you have ever been in your life. You are earning and receiving a thousand per month and your dream is a reality. The Count to Four Technique has worked for you and made it possible for you to almost triple your standard of living. It will help you to be anything you want to be and have anything you want to have.

Another example: A friend of mine is a man who, prior to three years ago, had never been in the direct selling field. He had been operating a modest dry cleaning business.

When I met him three years ago, he was a presser in a department store earning and receiving exactly $100 per week. He had never been before a group to make a talk at the time I met him. He had a 10th grade education, but like so many of us had not learned how to use the best of grammar as far as so-called correct speech was concerned. This man attended one of my lectures about three years ago, and he decided to do everything I asked him to do as I promised that he could be anything he wanted to be and that he could have anything he wanted to have.

In just three short years, he is a top sales executive of one of the most outstanding sales organizations in the world. His duties take him on lecture tours all over the United States, Canada, Hawaii and Alaska and soon he will go to Europe, Asia, Australia, New Zealand and Africa. He interviews the biggest people wherever he goes and his income is very substantial and is going up each year. He has everything he could desire. He lives in the finest suites at the finest hotels all over the world.

If You Can Count to Four - 18

He can do anything he desires because he has self confidence and an adequate amount of money.

Another example: About two years ago, I was lecturing along this line to a group of about 60 people near Los Angeles. Most of this small group were middle aged and older women in the selling field. I told them about the principles behind The Count to Four Technique. It was, as some of them told me later, just too good to be true. They wanted to believe it, but just found it impossible.

I felt this feeling among these very fine woman and I stopped right there on the spot and used The Count to Four Technique to help me to help them believe. I got the answer on the spot. I asked if there was at least one lady present, who is never, at any time, even secretly considered the idea of owning and casually driving a late model Cadillac automobile.

A charming lady raised her hand. In fact, several raised their hands, but I picked this one out as an example. I also asked her if she had an expensive dress. She said no, but that she would like one since I mentioned that she can have anything she wanted. Also, she said she was living in an apartment, which was very modest, that cost her about $30 per month. She was driving a used compact car, which at the time was worth about three-hundred and seventy-five dollars. I think that you all can get the picture.

Now, I told the group that in six months or less, this lady would own and be driving a late model Cadillac, be wearing a new expensive knit dress, and would be living in a new and expensive apartment comparable to her new way of life. They all looked goggle-eyed at me as though to say, "Can this really be true or is he a fool?"

Not six months later, but just 5 and one-half weeks later, this lady had her late model Cadillac, her knit dress and her new apartment. And all that she did was use what I have asked you to do in The Count to Four Technique.

She got well long into the plan, and after a week or so her subconscious mind began asking, "How can I earn and receive more money, because now I am a Cadillac girl and not a second-hand compact car girl. I'm a knit dress girl now, and I am a girl who lives in a new expensive apartment with period furniture. I want to find a way so I can be of greater service to

If You Can Count to Four - 19

humanity so that I can receive more compensation so I can comfortably live by my new standard."

Well, this lady's self-confidence and her sales increased so that she jumped from where she was at the time of the first lecture, to where she was just 5 and one-half weeks later. That has been a little less than two years ago, and now, I still know this very nice lady and at this time she is looking at a brand-new Cadillac. By the way, along with all the things which I mentioned, she also grew in poise, self-confidence, charm, patience, love of service, generosity, and many other very desirable mental attributes.

Her income today is at least three times what it was two years ago. Her self-confidence is 10 times what it was two years ago, and all because she decided to let me experiment in her case. She did not know exactly how it was going to happen, but she had confidence in me and did just exactly what I asked her to do. You say, "Yeah, he tells us these things, but he doesn't give us their names and addresses." If all you need, to believe this enough to try it, is to be able to contact this lady and ask her if I am telling you the truth, I'll be happy to give you names and addresses.

The way to state the Phase Four principle is this:

The size and color of your thoughts are cause. Your experiences are effect.

Each thought has size and color or quality and quantity. Your thought regarding income is cause. Your income is effect.

If you could go through some sort of mental exercise and thereby increase the quality and quantity of your thought, which is cause, soon the income, which is effect, would be increased accordingly.

The Count to Four Technique is a mental exercise, which expands our thoughts regarding our desires and the law of cause and effect brings our desires to pass.

You ask Mr. A. how much his income is at present, and he tells you that it is $400 per month. You ask him what kind of a house he lives in, and he tells you he lives in a $75 per month house. You ask him why he doesn't live in a $200 per month house, on a $400 per month income.

If You Can Count to Four - 20

Let's assume that he wants, very much, to live in a certain house which he can obtain for $200 per month. Let's now further assume that he goes to night school and gets a new job, where his services are now worth $650 per month instead of $400 per month. Now he obtains the $200 per month house and lives in it.

How much does it cost him? We will all have to admit that all he did was to increase the quality and quantity of his "thoughts" and this resulted in his 40 hours per week being worth $650 per month instead of the $400 earned previously. So, it didn't cost him anything to move into the $200 per month house from the $75 per month house.

Please try to think this through until it really means something to you. I know men who used to work very hard for $400 per month.

They worked hard for over 40 hours per week. Now they have so increased the value of their services per hour, that they work fewer hours, expand less energy and they are earning and receiving $4000 per month. I can take any man or woman, regardless of station in life, and if they will follow The Count to Four Technique, they can increase the quality and quantity of their "thoughts" and thereby increase the value of their services.

In turn, they will increase the amount of their income, and they can then obtain what they want. The Count to Four Technique will work for you regardless of whether your present income is $20 per week or $2000 per week. It is a principle which will make it possible for anyone, in any station in life, to merely decide what he wants to be and to have and then become it and have it.

It is now time that every person in the whole world should be told that success is just as simple as one, two, three, four. It is not as complicated as we have been told for centuries. It is good to get a formal education and to know as much as you can.

We have been told, however, that an education is indispensable and absolutely necessary before one can be successful. That is not so.

"If you can count to four", you can be anything you want to be and can have anything you want to have.

If You Can Count to Four - 21

I know this to be true, and I challenge anyone to prove me wrong!

2 - The Secret of Genuine Success

I wonder whether you have made some of the same observations I have made? From childhood, I always wondered why so many people in the community were not as prosperous as, apparently, they deserved. At the same time, a few people seemed to have everything. They seemed to have learned the secret of enjoying life. They also enjoyed a large measure of health, and I also noticed particularly, at that time, and at my level of appreciation, that they were enjoying a large measure of prosperity.

I asked myself the question why so many were not getting the best out of life and why so few had found the apparent secret. I decided to try to find the answer quite early in my life, and in a small way, I began my research. After graduating from high school, I began a planned and organized research. Over a period of 25 years, and I did special research on what I choose to call the practical aspects of psychology. It was my privilege to discover the answer to this problem and I would like to share it with you.

Before I give you the answer, however, I would like to make this observation. From the beginning I knew about this secret of success. I found also that the majority of the people actually have known about this secret all of their lives, but I found that even though I knew about it, and even though I found that everyone knew about it, very few of them knew it in such a way that they could take it into their lives and use it in a practical way. In other words, people knew about it, but, were not able to express it.

They were not enjoying a measure of happiness, health and prosperity, and as they deserved, and would be enjoying, if they knew how to use this secret. And thus I want to define this secret so you will not just know about it, but you will know it so well that you can use this principle and make it a habit in your everyday experience of living.

I would like first to illustrate the difference between knowing about something, and actually knowing it and living it. So you automatically use it in every expression of your daily living. A certain man is a lifeguard at a large swimming pool, approximately 100 feet long. He has developed such proficiency as a swimmer that he can swim the length of the pool over 50

If You Can Count to Four - 23

times without stopping. That would be a mile. He has also the ability to rescue those who are in trouble. He has the strength, power and technique as a swimmer, and can truly stand up and say, "I am a swimmer."

However, another man is a very proficient lecturer on swimming. He has large classes where he lectures on the techniques of swimming. He knows all of the strokes. In the classroom, he has grace and charm in his ability to describe all of the intimate techniques of swimming.

One day, one of the students asked this professor where he learned to swim.

He replied that he had learned to swim in the library.

Now I ask you, which one of these gentlemen would you like to be with when your boat turned over in deep water? You would choose the one who is the lifeguard at the swimming pool, who can swim 50 laps without any trouble at all and who can rescue you. I am sure you would choose him because he is a swimmer. Every cell in his body has been saturated with an awareness of all of the techniques of swimming, and he has proved, by experience, that he can swim. He has strength and power and knowledge of swimming. He can do the things he teaches as a matter of habit. But the professor only knows about it, can tell you all about it, but he cannot do it.

Now, in this thing called success, it has been my privilege to observe that most people are just like the professor who learned about swimming in the library. Yes, the majority of people, relative to success, are in the same position as the professor. They know all about success, but they are not successful.

They are frustrated and emotionally disturbed. They are filled with fears and worries and concerns and anxieties, and life does not mean a great deal to them because it expresses itself in terms of disharmony and frustration. But if they knew not only how to be successful and if they practice the rules of success, which are available to all people today, they would soon learn to be happy in a tangible fashion just as the swimmer learned to swim. But many of us are still trying to be successful, like the swimmer who wants to be a swimmer, but never gets in the water.

If You Can Count to Four - 24

So, in my own case, this quest started many, many years ago. I wanted to know why so many people knew about success, but so few people were successful. I would like to pass the answer I discovered on to you. The answer is that any individual, on the face of this earth, can be genuinely happy, genuinely healthy and a genuinely prosperous if he will do just one thing.

Switch is focal point of attention from "How much can I get out of life?" and developed a habitual concern about, "How much can I give?"

In other words, *any individual on the face of the earth can be happy, healthy and prosperous if he will seek an opportunity to serve where there is an unlimited opportunity to serve humanity.*

He must find that particular channel, which he seems to have been designed to serve through, and then get into that channel of service, where there is a genuine need, where there is a genuine opportunity to serve. Then, he must become proficient and learn to render, first of all, a quality of service, which means integrity and know-how.

After he has learned to render a quality of service, he must learn to render a *quantity* of service. Of course, he will be compensated according to the quality and quantity of service rendered. He will be compensated in two ways.

The first compensation that I would like to share with you is a compensation that has meant more to me than any other I have ever experienced. That is the feeling of satisfaction I experience from having gone out with one idea in mind, in my daily activities, and finding an opportunity to render a real, genuine service without any thought of financial remuneration as the number one motive. That feeling of satisfaction I choose to call "livingness."

This "livingness" - this feeling of real satisfaction, once experienced, through switching your focal point of attention from being interested in making money to rendering a genuine service to humanity, will be a revelation to you. Your "livingness" with this genuinely felt adjustment and focal point will not be worthy to be compared with the so-called thrill of making money, but, a switch of focal point from making money as a prime motive to one of genuine service reaps a more satisfying return to you.

If You Can Count to Four - 25

The first compensation, to one who has dedicated himself to this secret of success of rendering a great service to humanity, is "livingness."

Of course, the great universal law of compensation proves to us that *we are compensated, in the coin of the realm, according to the quality and the quantity of service rendered*, and I would like to say that this law of success is not a theory.

I will never teach anything which is based upon a theory. Everything that I want to share with you is based upon scientific research and experience.

Now, this idea of switching our focal point of attention from seeking money, power and fame – seeking first to render a quality and a quantity of service to humanity – is based upon a system of laws and rules as tangible as mathematics, as tangible as electricity, as tangible as chemistry itself.

We all know that mathematics, electricity, and the chemistry are sciences which are tangible and exact. An electrician can come into your home and wire your building and he can tell you that a certain light will burn, and that your television set will work, and that every electrical appliance will work according to an exact science.

Men and women study for months and years learning this exact science known as electricity. We all know that mathematics is also an exact science. We all know that chemistry is an exact science. I have found that most people are like I have been most of my life.

They do not realize that success and thinking are also based upon an exact science, a set of rules, a set of laws which any individual who is sincerely seeking the answer to the problems of frustration and ill health and poverty can study. They can study these rules, as electricians study electricity, and as a mathematician studies mathematics. They can learn these rules and practice them until they become automatic through the law habit. Doing this will guarantee them a large measure of happiness, health and prosperity, according to their individuality.

I would like to challenge each and every one of you to realize that it is possible for you to be anything that you want to be and to have anything that you want to have. I know that for many of

If You Can Count to Four - 26

you that will seem like a truly bold statement. It may seem a bit revolutionary to some of you.

But I would like you to know that I come from the Hill section of the great state of Tennessee. I was born into a family of 14 children and had a background of relative poverty. I look back and I am grateful for that humble beginning. I feel very thankful because it provided the drive for me to discover the secret of success.

I can truthfully say that I know from experience, as well as many years of scientific research in this realm known as the thought processes, that you can be anything that you want to be and that you can have anything that you want to have. This is based upon a scientific set of rules which you can learn just as easily as you're A, B, C's and your multiplication tables.

I would like to urge each and every one of you to accept this challenge and to begin to think definitely in terms of what you want to be. I could tell you story after story of students of mine who have made lists of things that they want to be.

In fact, just recently, I was having my shoes shined at the shoe shine parlor, outside the television studio, and there was a very fine young man who shined my shoes. In discussing this idea of success with him briefly, I told him that he could be anything that he wants to be or that he could have anything that he wants to have. He was rather amazed.

He said, "You mean to tell me that I can have anything that I want to have and that I can be anything I want to be?" I said, "Absolutely, and what do you want to be?" He said, "I want to be a great comedian. A combination of master of ceremonies and a great comedian." I said, "You really mean that, young fellow?" He said, "I certainly do. I want to be that more than anything else in the world." I said, "You can be it." He asked, "How in the world can I be it? I'm nobody."

I explained to him briefly, how to go about it, that the first thing he should do is to realize that there is a system of rules and scientific principles upon which success is based. Then I briefly explained to him that he has the capacity to imagine himself a great success in his chosen field, and that it is his privilege to design his own success. As he exercises his tremendous faculty that is within him, and each of us, with the capacity to imagine what we want to be developed, and we are

If You Can Count to Four - 27

able to design our own success through this wonderful faculty of imagination.

I went ahead and, in much detail, to describe to him the "one, two, three, four formula." He was rather amazed and I was very pleased, indeed, when I felt that he had accepted it and he intended to begin immediately to do something about it. He believed, after a few suggestions, that he could be this great comedian and master of ceremonies.

I predict that, in the years to come, you will hear of this young man in the various entertainment circles of the world because he is now visualizing himself as being what he wants to be and having what he wants to have. Having visualized it, he will be driven to do something about becoming more proficient in his work. That will assure his success.

As I have said, the answer to this problem of health and happiness and prosperity is not a theory, but it is tangible. It is based upon sound laws and the challenge to everyone is to accept this and to make a study of it. It is my desire and privilege to share these wonderful true facts based upon this exact science with you, which will help you to become what you want to become and to have everything that you want to have.

The secret of genuine success is very simple. All you have to do is to find a great channel of service to humanity.

Choose that particular channel, of course, for which you seem to be especially designed because there are many, many channels of service to humanity. There are many, many genuine needs. People need thousands of things.

I would like to point out a rather tangible observation that I have made. If you stop and think, you too, would have made the same observation. Every man and woman, in history, who has ever had his or her name recorded in the history books, is there because he or she either consciously or unconsciously discovered this one principle of success. He or she found a channel of service to humanity, which was genuine and that channel of service which he or she seemed to have been especially adapted. After they chose that channel, they learn to render a quality and quantity of service to humanity.

I mention men like Thomas A. Edison and Henry Ford, and some contemporary people right now on the American scene - Henry Kaiser, R. G. La Tourneau and quite a number of

If You Can Count to Four - 28

outstanding men and women in every realm of life, in industry, in statesmanship and in religion. All of these great men and women have become historically important, And currently important, because they have learned the secret of rendering a quality and a quantity of service to humanity.

I would like to say that it is your privilege, not only to be what you want to be, but it is your privilege to have anything that you want to have. I would like to stress that it is most important, in the early stages of your research into this field, to make a list of all the things that you want to be, first, then make a list of all the things that you want to have. I would like to suggest that you start on the road to genuine success by doing this immediately. Take a note book and on one half of a page, list all of the things that you would like to be.

Would you like to be a person of greater poise? Would you like to be a person known in the community as a person who always expresses kindness in every situation?

Would you like to be known as a person of charm and a person who was always aware of the good, the true and the beautiful? These are qualities which can be studied and practiced until the law of habit takes over and you automatically are kind and cultured and aware of the good and the true and the beautiful in every situation.

We certainly know lots of people nowadays, who seem to be seeing that which is other than good and true and beautiful because they are discouraged and sad and frustrated and are expressing themselves inadequately compared to the complete life, which is theirs and they could discover this great secret.

Make a list of all the things that you want to be. This great principle of which I speak is unlimited in its scope. You can be anything that you want to be. If you want to be a great singer, began to imagine that you are already a great singer. Put that on your list.

Now, over on the other side of the page, may I suggest that you begin to list all of the things that you want to have. Would you like to have a better home? Would you like to have a larger and more spacious and livable home?

There is enough material in this universe to build a mansion for every living soul upon the face of the earth. We have an absolutely inexhaustible supply.

If You Can Count to Four - 29

There is a system of rules for utilizing the supply, which I will share with you. I would like to suggest, most strongly, that when each of you realize that *when you see limitations in your own individual lives and limitations in the lives of others, it is not because there is no adequate supply to fill your needs. It is because you are unable to understand the method of appropriating this infinite supply.*

List all of the things that you want to have, a beautiful home, a beautiful automobile, clothes and all of the things that you want to be, then read it over constantly. Change it as your desires change, and you will see marvelous changes happen almost immediately in your life.

I challenge you to learn the secret of success, to find a great channel of service to humanity, and then render it in a quality and quantity, and you can be anything you want to be, you can have anything you want to have.

3 - Awareness Is Power!

We have considered the secret of genuine success in general. Now, let us consider some of the ABC's of building a state of beingness so that success will become habitual or automatic and our lives.

We can refer to these ABC's as the four simple rules of success.

There are four basic fundamental ideas which I would like to share with each of you. May I suggest that you get a notebook and write these rules or ideas down so they can become part of your being. This will be of tangible help to each of you in starting to make you be anything you want to be and have anything you want to have.

So, the **first rule** that I would like to share with you is this: *We must become aware of the fact that we are thinking beings.*

Of all of God's creations, we are the only part of the entire universe that has the privilege of thinking. And naturally when we think of thinking, we become aware that we are dealing with mental processes.

I would like to have you become keenly aware that you are thinking all the time, that you are a thinking being, that you have what is known in psychology as mental processes, and you, if you will stop and take inventory, will recognize that these thought processes surging through your being.

Make a special note in your notebook and say to yourself, "I am a thinking being; I am constantly thinking thoughts; I am constantly having a mental process during every waking hour, every waking moment and every waking split second."

You are consciously having a thought process and, of course, at night, while you are asleep, your subconscious mind is always active; expressing itself in the form of a thought process. So, number one of these rules, which are so fundamental and very important for you to remember, is to constantly be aware that you are thinking.

Rule number two is to *be aware that you can only think one thought at a time.*

I remember very well when I first became aware that I was a thinking being, and it was suggested that I can think only one thought at a time. I thought, "No, I could think two or three or four thoughts at a time." I was wrong. You and I can think only one thought at a time. It only seems that we can think more than one thought at a time.

Our ability to switch our attention so frequently and so rapidly causes us to have the illusion that we are thinking more than one thought at a time. So, let us be keenly aware that we are thinking beings, that we have thought processes, and that we cannot think two thoughts or three thoughts at a time, but we can think only one thought at a time.

Rule number three is that *we must be keenly aware not only of the fact that we can think only one thought at a time but that we can control all of our thought processes.*

We can control each single thought we have. I believe that most of us have been under the false illusion that we cannot control our thinking. Most of us believe that outside forces, the power of suggestion from a friend, reading something in a newspaper, or listening to something on the radio or television overpowers our thinking processes and causes us to think thoughts that are undesirable, untrue, and ugly.

Let me assure you, that you have within you the power to control every thought that you think. Yes, you are thinking constantly, you can think only one thought at a time and you can control your thinking. Regardless of the situation, regardless of how hard the situation may be, you have the power and the privilege of reacting to that situation as you choose by controlling the thoughts which you think, one at a time.

I would like to elaborate upon this because it is so important to our health of body and of mind, our feeling of well-being and to our success. I was happy, indeed, happy to discover that I had the privilege of either reacting positively or reacting negatively to any given situation.

Yes, I was in control, regardless of the appearance of the situation which might appear as a tragedy, which might appear as a situation that would cause the average person to be discouraged, frustrated and upset, and negatively excited.

This realization came as a natural result of understanding that I was a thinking being, that I had thought processes constantly, that I could think only one thought at a time, and that I could

If You Can Count to Four - 32

control the one thought which I was thinking at any given split-second of time.

I suddenly realized that because of this I had the power to control my reaction to each situation. I suddenly realized that, in the last and ultimate analysis, no situation had the power to disturb me if I refused to be disturbed; that no situation had the power to discourage me if I refused to be discouraged.

I found that I could not experience discouragements, unless I permitted myself to think discouraging thoughts. I found that the basic thought process, thinking one thought at a time, is the basis of control of every situation; that the situation itself has no power.

Situations which appear to be tragedies, situations which appear to be disappointments and discouragements, cause the average person to be upset, unhappy, frustrated and miserable, and many times ill.

Think of what a tremendous discovery it is when you become keenly aware that a situation has absolutely no power, no power whatsoever over us individually. Yes, you can be master of every situation when you know for certain that you are a thinking being and that you can think only one thought at a time, and that you can control every single thought.

That conclusion may seem, at first, to be untrue and unbelievable. If it seems to be untrue to you, that feeling you have is based upon the fact that you have established a habit pattern in your subconscious mind, would causes you to react habitually to various situations in a negative way.

If you almost always seem to be thinking wrong thoughts, if you almost always seem to be discouraged in certain situations, if you seem to be frustrated and react negatively over and over and over, you have developed a negative habit.

Even though you now have discovered that it is your privilege to react and control any situation, you will continue to react as you formerly did. For a little while you may have a little difficulty establishing a new habit pattern of developing control and guiding your reactions to every situation toward to seeing the good, the true and the beautiful.

Soon, in every situation, because you can control your thinking, you will begin to look for that which is good before you react,

If You Can Count to Four - 33

and you will say to yourself, "I refuse to react in any situation spontaneously until I have given sufficient thought to it. And until I have evaluated that situation sufficiently to permit me to see something good in the situation, and I refuse to react until I can say something good about that situation."

I think, perhaps, at this time, it would be well to dwell a little bit on "will power." Many people believe that will power is the thinking which causes people to be successful.

Many people say, "I am going to be successful even if it kills me." Well, in many cases, it does that very thing.

I would like to tell you a little story that will give you some idea of the function of will power in our lives. Let us suppose that we're going to build a table top, a beautiful table top, and we have all the finished boards ready to assemble as the top. We are going to glue those boards together, so we secure a glue that is especially prepared for this job. We apply the glue, then we put the boards together. Then, we put the clamps on the boards to hold them together until the glue dries. We know that it takes a certain minimum amount of time for this glue to go through a prescribed drying process before it will hold strongly enough to allow for removing the clamps.

Now, the will power in this situation is illustrated by the clamps. The clamps hold the boards in place until another power in the glue has time to take hold so the boards will stay together without the help of the clamps.

In our mental processes, we decide that we are going to establish a new idea. Then, we proceed to form that new idea into a habit so it will automatically cause us to react to every future situation in harmony with our new being and our new principle. But realizing that the old habits are well established, and we react automatically according to our old habits, we have to work diligently to establish this new habit.

The only way we can establish this new habit pattern is through control of our thinking, the use of our will power. *Through will power, we clamp our new thoughts, our new concepts, our new objectives, our new desires, even though they are in conflict with the old habits, with the will power and hold them in place until we have the new habit established so strongly that it neutralizes the old habit.*

If You Can Count to Four - 34

Soon, the old habit then has no further power over us, and we automatically, having clamped that new thought in place, hold the thoughts in place until the glue has dried. When we first think of an idea it is like the newly applied glue.

It is a little bit difficult to hold in place, but, when we clamp it there with the will power and refuse to think any thoughts contrary to our new ideas until our new idea becomes permanently established and becomes a strong habit pattern, we can take off the clamps.

The will power and our thoughts will stay in place and we automatically interpret every situation with the proper reaction. We will react with courage instead of discouragement; and we will react with faith instead of doubt, and we will see the beauty in the situation instead of ugliness. We will see the good in every situation instead of that which appears to be otherwise.

Because a major point of determine this discovery I want to share with you is, that it is your privilege to think and to control your thinking, to the point where you can design anything that you want to be and anything that you want to have.

As a new idea, let us definitize it. You realize that, at the outset, your thoughts about the new concept of yourself, which you have designed, are either hazy or are definite in design.

You can think of yourself as being a person of poise, a person of courage, a person of faith, a person of great stick-to-it-iveness, a person of great stability, of kindness and love and service and understanding.

All of those thoughts actually have definite size and color and quality. How you see it at the outset is of no consequence, because through the use of will power, you can hold your attention and control one thought at a time and direct it toward that which you want to be until you become that.

As soon as you have this habit pattern of new thoughts well established in your subconscious, you will suddenly realize that you are the thing that you want to be, the person that you want to be. Then, when you begin to direct your thinking, one thought at a time, to incorporate possessing that which you want to possess, you build what we call acceptance of the new thought or idea in the subconscious mind.

If You Can Count to Four - 35

You embody, you design, you build a mental mood for controlling this new idea with will power until this new design becomes established as a habit pattern. Soon, this embodied idea, this well defined idea, controlled through will power, becomes firmly established, until you have what we call full acceptance. Then, you will suddenly realize that the very physical equivalent of the idea has appeared in your own individual life.

Rule number four: *I would like for you to realize, that what we are at this time, is the result of everything we have thought throughout our entire past.*

Our loveliness or unloveliness, our kindness or our tendency toward unkindness, our faith for our tendency toward doubt, everything that we are, is the result of our past thoughts.

Whether we are persons of confidence or persons of timidity, whether we are persons of courage or persons who are easily discouraged, whether we are persons of poise or whether we are persons who feel ill at ease in life's situations, whether we are persons of integrity or whether we are persons who lack integrity, we are what we are, you are what you are, I am what I am, he is what he is because of the thoughts which we have permitted ourselves to think throughout the entire past.

If I might quote the great Solomon of old, who said that, "As a man thinketh in his heart, so is he."

Note this. What Solomon said about a man being what he thinks in his heart is not true because Solomon said it. Solomon said it because it is true. It means something to us today, not because someone said it many years ago, but, because it is true.

Another great teacher of old said that, "Ye shall know the truth and the truth shall make you free." We know that we can seek the truth about ourselves and through the control of our thought processes, chart our future.

You, I am sure, feel the same way I felt most of my life. That something else has caused me to be what I am. I have a friend who believes that the climatic conditions and the political situations and some distorted, demented uncle or aunt is to blame for his predicament. In fact, this friend of mine can tell me a dozen reasons why he is not happy and why he is in need of money constantly.

If You Can Count to Four - 36

But it has never occurred to this friend of mine that he is the cause of his present situation, that he has been unaware of the fact that he has a thinking process, that he has a thought process constantly every waking hour, and that the thoughts which he permits himself to think during the day, the subconscious thinks all night long, and gradually he becomes that which he has permitted himself to think.

Thus, he is the cause of his present situation of unhappiness and poverty. He does not realize that it is his privilege to redirect his thought process to control his thoughts, and inasmuch as each thought is a well-defined concept or idea, through the control of his thought processes, he can redesign himself to be anything that he wants to be.

I want to emphasize the basic fact that whatever you are and whatever I am and whatever he is, we are what we are because of the thoughts which we have permitted ourselves to think.

There is absolutely nothing on the outside of us that has any power over us if we will not permit it. We would never have thoughts which cause us to react in a negative fashion, cause us to think thoughts that we do not want to have, if we could possibly visualize the quality of thought.

Also, we should be keenly aware of the fact that whatever we want to be and whatever we want to have, we can be all of the wonderful things we want to be and we can have all of the wonderful things we want to have

- by realizing that we are thinking beings, that we can think only one thought at a time,
- that we can control this thought process by directing our will power towards that which we want to be until it becomes a habit,
- that we are what we are today because of all of the thoughts which we have thought throughout all of the past.

This discovery will cause us to be aware that there is a system of rules which operate according to an exact science. By defining clearly the things we want to be and the things we want to have, through control and direction of our attention units along those lines, we can become anything that we want to become and we can have anything we want to have.

If You Can Count to Four - 37

Isn't it a marvelous thing to become aware of these wonderful things? Isn't it marvelous to realize it is really up to us to literally design our future, so we can be anything we want to be and we can have anything we want to have, regardless of the scope?

I challenge you to think largely and to make large plans, because they have magic to stir man's blood.

Continue to make that list of the things you want to be and make a list of all the things you want to have.

Begin to realize that they all can be yours by being aware that you are a thinking being, that you have a thought process, that you can think only one thought at a time, that you can control this thought process through will power, that you are what you are because of this and that **you can be anything you want to be and that you can have anything you want to have.**

4 - Choosing Your Goal

How many people do you imagine know what they want to be in life? How many know what they want to have?

Oh, in a general sense, most everyone has some hazy idea that they want to be famous, important, happy, successful, etc., but it was a shock to me to discover that less than 2% of the people know to any definite degree what they want to be and what they want to have. 98 out of every 100 have not done any clear, distinct, definitized thinking regarding their beingness or havingness.

You may ask the question, why? Why is it that so few have gotten around to defining their goals? Why so many have drifted along with the tide of humanity? Well, it would take many pages to give you the deeper answer, but briefly, at this point, the reason is that only a few or a where is that "thinking" has anything to do with what happens to them.

There are a few basic facts regarding the way the mind functions which I would like to explore with you at this point in our consideration.

You see, our mind, even though it is one, seems to function through two major phases. These two phases, we call the conscious and the subconscious. The conscious phase is the part of us, which is aware, and is the personal and male part of the mind. The subconscious is the impersonal and female part and is not aware.

The conscious phase is the part of us that can say, "I AM." When you say, "I am happy," or "I am healthy," or "I am successful," or "I am displeased," or "I am at home," or "I am sick," or "I am poor," or "I am unhappy." Any such remark, which means that you are aware of some state of beingness is the function of your conscious mind.

Our Creator especially designed us so that we can reason. We can reason either deductively or inductively. But I remembered just how difficult those words were for meat the outset, so instead of calling the two functions of reason deductive and inductive reasoning, with your permission, I will refer to them as the "A" type and "B" type of reasoning.

If You Can Count to Four - 39

Our conscious mind has the ability of reason either "A" type or "B" type.

- "A" type means that we have the ability to investigate any matter, remark or situation before we will accept it as true.
- "B" type means that we have within us the ability to accept it as true on the assumption that it is true without having investigated it.

The subconscious mind has the ability to reason, only according to the "B" type. It cannot investigate, it accepts whatever the conscious mind tells it and accepts it as being true. But once the subconscious accepts anything as true, even though it may be untrue, it begins right away to arrange itself so that whatever it has accepted appears to be true. So it is our privilege to investigate everything that comes our way, that we may know it is true, before we accept it as a part of our beliefs.

That's me say with all the strength of my beingness, that I believe that one of the most important phases of the entire study of life. Is this phase dealing with the "A" and "B" type reasoning of the two major phases of our minds. Most of the misunderstandings of the ages stem from not understanding how the mind functions in regard to its reasoning processes.

After much sincere and devoted research in this field, I now believe that unless one understands the simple ABC rules of the way the mind functions, one cannot be sure of anything he believes.

For example, before a certain period in the history of the earth, everybody, including the most respected scientists, believe that the earth was flat. No one had ever investigated it. It appeared to be flat to everyone. The leading scientist of the day could give you good, seemingly reliable reasons why it was flat. Why is this possible? How could these scientists be so mistaken? He had used the "B" type reasoning and had assumed that it was flat because it looked like it was flat. He had not used the "A" type reasoning, which made it possible to really investigate it.

But just as soon as a Columbus came along and dared to go beyond what had been done before, and his research proved that the Earth was not flat, but round, the scientists announced the new discovery, and then the millions accepted the new concept on the assumption that they have now found the truth. But the millions used only the "B" type of reasoning.

The above example seems to prove conclusively that it is possible for us to be living on a false premise of values, even though every bit of evidence which we have tends to prove that we are right.

But isn't it a marvelous thing to know that now we can take everything that we presently believe and put it upon the table of investigation and find out the genuine truth about it by using the "A" type of reasoning.

Let me say, that in my own personal experience, I have found that when things were not going well in some phase of my life, I later found out that it was because I was not aware of the truth regarding that phase. When I learned the truth about that phase, things became harmonious and satisfactory.

Now, due to the nature of the functions of the two major phases of the mind, *98% of the people do not understand the way the mind works*. They are the victims of every suggestion which comes their way. Whether it comes from a friend, a parent, a minister, radio, television or newspapers. They do not know that, whatever impresses the conscious, and in turn impresses the subconscious, must express itself in their lives as an experience.

Each idea of which we conceive in the conscious mind is like a seed in the vegetable realm. If we believe it, and impress it upon our subconscious, it is like planting a seed in good soil. The subconscious is the womb of life, like the soil is the womb of the vegetable realm and the proton is the womb of the mineral realm. The challenge is to become as familiar with the "thought" realm as we are with the animal, the vegetable and the mineral realms.

In the "thought" realm, the idea concept is the father. The subconscious is the mother, and the result is the son.

Now, we are all exercising this great law at every waking moment. Whatever we permit ourselves to give our attention units to, we appropriate the law of sowing and reaping in the realm of "thought." Now, since this is true, we can well understand that throughout all the past, we have all been giving our attention to something during every waking moment. And

If You Can Count to Four - 41

since the law says that we reap what we sow, we have been reaping, in our daily experiences, the result of our sowings.

Maybe you will say, "I didn't realize that I sowed the type of seed that would bring me such a harvest as this." But as I said before, many of us are not aware that we are sowing, but it doesn't matter whether we are aware of it or not, we put the law in motion when we give our attention to either the lovely or the unlovely and we must reap the harvest after its kind.

Now we know that we are thinking beings. We also know that we can think only one thought at a time. We know that we can control this talk, which searches through our beingness. We can direct it in any direction we choose. We can design the type of experiences we desire to express. We can determine just what we want to be and half, and the entire universe, with all its power, wisdom and unlimited resources is behind us to help us attain our goal.

Every man and woman in history, who has received any recognition, has consciously or unconsciously directed his or her attention toward a goal of his or her own choosing, and by controlling his or her attention, he or she invoked the infinite powers of the universe on his or her behalf.

Every book, it seems to me, that has been written on success, in recent years, tells the story of *Henry Ford, Thomas A. Edison, John Wannamaker, William Wrigley* and the familiar ones. It is true that the successful gentleman mentioned have chosen a definite goal, and used to the principles of success in order to attain them.

However, it is my desire to make it quite clear, that *anyone, regardless of who he may be, regardless of his station in life at the present time, can discover his goal in life and by directing his attention to it, can obtain it and live a very happy, healthy and prosperous life.*

It has been said that 98 people out of every 100 do not have a goal or main purpose in life. That is not true. Every person has a goal or a major purpose in life. Every person was especially designed to serve or express life in some particular channel well. 98 have not discovered their channel as yet.

The Bible tells us to: *"Ask, and it shall be given unto us;" "Seek, and ye shall find;" "Knock, and it shall be opened unto you."*

If You Can Count to Four - 42

Perhaps your goal, at this time, should be to find your main goal in life. Then ask that you be shown just what your major purpose in life is. Whom do you ask? Ask God. How do you ask God? God is infinite intelligence.

The subconscious phase of our mind is the channel through which we contact and infinite intelligence. When we have a movement of thought (controlled) in the conscious mind, the defined ideas contained in our thoughts are impressed upon the subconscious, which in turn, in its own way, takes it up with the infinite intelligence and the answer comes back just as tangibly as a telephone or a telegraph message.

The answer comes back through natural means. Sometimes, it comes through a person, sometimes through intuition. So, let each of us, who is still in the list with the 98, get busy and start asking infinite intelligence to tell us what our "big channel of service" is.

This works, I know, because I have been working it for years as casually as writing a letter or making a telephone call.

Now, soon, you will know what your goal in life is. Soon you will know what you want to be. Soon you will know how to appropriate all the wisdom, power, material, and ingredients and anything you desire in the invisible or the visible realm of life.

Because, when you have learned the tremendous power of directing your attention toward whatever you desire, you will begin the type of beingness and the type of havingness that you have secretly dreamed about all your life.

It is necessary that each of us decide what we want to be and what we want to have.

Until we definitely decide what our goal is, we will be confronted with the necessity of making a new decision every day of what our goal is for that particular day. Each night, before we go to sleep, we should design the pattern of our activities for the following day in terms of our goal.

When we do that, the subconscious is impressed and it works on that pattern all night while we are asleep. Then we seem to automatically do everything right all day the next day. The pattern which we design and take to bed with us is easy to follow the next day.

If You Can Count to Four - 43

But, if we neglect to design a desirable pattern, just before we go to bed, and unconsciously go to sleep with mood, we will go through the next day with a negative mood.

There is one exception to this. If you have a quiet time, early during the day, you can use your will power to neutralize your negative mood, and dynamically outline a positive pattern, on the spot, for the rest of the day.

1. So, first of all, we define our goals.
2. Then we must develop a strong feeling, or a "white heat" desire for our objectives.
3. The subconscious responds to our desires to the degree of our feeling impressed upon it.

How do we develop a "white heat" feeling regarding our objectives? But assuming how we would feel if we already were what we want to be or we already have what we desire to possess. Also, by visiting with a companion or a friend whom we know will be for us and who will share our joys of attainment.

Another very helpful technique is to obtain color pictures of what you want and put them on the wall by your bed, near the mirror, in the bathroom, and any other place where you will see them frequently.

May I share a personal experience with you, which will illustrate a very effective method of building a burning desire and a consciousness for something new? A few years ago, while I was in the insurance and investment business, our company issued a special 6 year annuity investment policy. Very few of our agents around the country sold much of it.

For the first three years I was with the company, I did not sell a single policy of that type. I had no feeling for it. I did not see its value. I had no desire to sell it and consequently did not sell it.

However, as an experiment, after discovering the principle of how my mind worked, I decided to use the principle and see what would happen. I obtained all the literature available on this policy, and each night, just before going to sleep, I read and studied the entire kit of literature thoroughly. I did that for about 30 nights.

If You Can Count to Four - 44

At the same time, I made a 15 minute recording on my record player and for the entire 15 minutes, I made statements from the assumption that I was an expert selling a minimum amount of this policy each week. I played this recording over and over each night and morning during this 30 day period.

Pretty soon, I began to see why certain men and women would want to invest their money in that plan. During the month that this took place, I wrote enough of this plan to earn $440 in commission.

During the following month, I earned $1200 on that one plan. I became an expert in presenting the plan to people who were able to invest large sums in that type of plan.

Note that, before I conditioned my mind, by reading the entire kit of literature over and over, each night for 30 nights, and playing the recording over and over to myself, I had known about the plan for three years, and yet had made no sales at all.

May I suggest to you, if you are selling something as a vocation, try the above experiment. Anything that you can devise that will help you to control your conscious attention is good, that is, if it is honest and does not harm anyone else.

Many people do the following.

1. They assume that they already have attained their objective and then plan to dramatize an event which could only take place if they have already attained their goal.

2. Then, they play this little drama, and the subconscious is impressed, because it is implied that they have are ready reach their goal.

We had a party at our house celebrating my debut on television about three months before my first television program. We assumed that we had just come from the studio and all of us were celebrating my first telecast. We all were in on the principle, and understood its power, and everyone was excited and congratulations were extended to me as though I had given a good lecture, etc.

That was three months before my first appearance on television, on June 19th. At that time, we did not know just when would be able to start the series of telecasts. We were using a known technique to impress our subconscious minds

If You Can Count to Four - 45

and developing a definitized, burning, obsessional desire for our goal. May I suggest that you get some friends to play the game with you. Have him or her shake your hand and congratulate you on having become the person you desire to be or having attained the goal you desire to obtain.

This applies to any quality of mind that you desire to have. It also applies to any type of expression, you might desire to experience, such as singing, traveling, golfing, etc.

This also applies to employment. It also applies to the size of your income. Get a notebook and begin to list the things that you want to be and have. You can change it as often as you wish, but you will soon find that your desires will begin to stabilize and you will soon feel strongly along certain lines.

Your real and genuine desires will come forth and you will be one of the 2% instead of one of the 98% who do not know what they want to be or what they want to have.

Let me challenge you to know that we live in an inexhaustible abundance in this universe. *There is no limit to what you can be or have, except your ability to dream and believe in your dream.*

"Make large plans, for they have magic to stir men's blood."

If You Can Count to Four - 46

5 - You Can Have Self-Confidence

I am wondering if you would like to have more self-confidence, and would like to get rid of all your feelings of inferiority? Well, that is exactly what is going to happen, provided you are sincerely interested and will follow a few suggestions.

It seems that most everyone has a degree of feeling of inferiority. So don't feel so exclusive about your complexes. You have lots of company. At the same time, most everyone feels very confident about certain things. Certain things, about which they have learned enough, so that they feel that they are an authority. All this proves that each of us has the capacity to feel confident as well as inferior. We feel confident when we understand the whole truth about something, and we feel inferior, when we do not know the whole truth.

Webster defines the word inferiority as a person experiencing a feeling in a lower state.

In other words, by feeling that somebody else is better than he is, he is comparing himself with this other person. This is not a fair comparison. No two persons are the same. The very word individual suggests that each one of us is different from every other person. We do not look the same as anyone else. We have a different shaped nose, face, head, body, and we have a different design as to what our life's purpose is.

We were designed to function as an individual. We are not to be compared with any other person, but we should appreciate our individual design and learn to be ourselves.

We should learn to express our own individuality well.

The one great Creator of the universe has infinite intelligence. Infinite intelligence means unlimited, incomprehensible, inexhaustible, wisdom, knowledge, and power.

The universe is designed, powered and governed by this all powerful, all knowing, all loving Creator. This indescrabable creator knows that it takes thousands of different types of individuals to render all the many different services needed to operate the world harmoniously, so he created thousands of different types of people. There are thousands of men who just love to serve as undertakers. Other thousands of men who like to run grocery stores. Others who like to sell and deal with people. Others, who like to be statesmen and run our government.

Why this great intelligence, which runs the universe, has it arranged that should the one and only undertaker in some little town in western Nebraska gets killed in an auto accident, in three days, there would be several other undertakers competing for the opportunity to serve in his place.

Did you ever wonder how it is possible for every city and community in the world, based upon its population, to have just the right number of doctors, lawyers, merchants, plumbers, carpenters, ditch diggers, ministers, salesman, nurses, lawnmower repairers, waiters, cooks, mechanics, etc.? Why is it that just so many persons trained to render each type of service live in each community?

That happens because each of us is especially designed to serve well in some channel. We develop our abilities to serve in our particular channel, and then seek a place where such services are needed.

When we find our channel, the channel for which we were especially created, we will find that we are very happy serving in that channel. We will feel harmonious and happy, and we will express life beautifully. We will be healthy and prosperous because we will find that we will be able to render a quality and a quantity of service to humanity. We will have faith in ourselves and will not be comparing ourselves with other people who were designed to serve in a different channel than ourselves.

You will pardon me if I share a personal experience with you. I was raised in a family of 14 children. There are 12 of us living at present. Most of my life, I suffered terribly from a feeling of inferiority. I did not understand why other people could have so many desirable things and be playing seemingly such an important role in life. And I seemed to be stuck with wearing hand-me-downs, and plowing with a walking plow all my life. I felt inferior to every boy who wore better clothes than I did. I felt inferior to every boy or girl who could stand up before the student body and speak with poise and confidence.

I could not do that when I was a senior in high school. I felt inferior to every boy and girl who seemed to feel at ease at the socials, which I attended during my school years, because I

If You Can Count to Four - 48

came from the sticks and looked and dressed like a hayseed. During those years, I did not understand the real foundation of life. I did not know what was important and what was unimportant.

But looking back, I can see many things about those years, which turned out to be blessings in disguise. Two things I will mention.

One, these conditions stirred within me a burning desire to learn the truth about life and to be successful.

Two, since I did not have the clothes, the money, and the confidence, so that I was invited to the many social activities, I took my borrowed books and went home and did the chores and studied each evening until bedtime. Consequently, I learned to study and made good grades. I learned the value of knowing the truth about that which I was studying.

My confidence gradually grew and grew, as I learned the truth about the universe and its various laws. It has been my privilege to take all these wonderful discoveries out into the test tube of life and prove them. Now, I know that each person can discover that channel for which he was especially designed and learn to express a large measure of happiness, health and prosperity.

I would like to introduce a wonderful word to you, which will mean a great deal to your happiness. The word is "consciousness." It means the sum total of all your beliefs.

Add up every thought or idea which you have ever accepted as true and that adds up to your state of beingness or consciousness.

If you have accepted thoughts in the past which are not true, regarding who you are and what your relationship to other people is, then you have a consciousness of inferiority. You have that consciousness because you have accepted certain untrue things as though they were true.

If you knew the truth about yourself you would not feel inferior, but you would jump up and down and shout. You would know that your Creator is richer than Henry Ford, and he is smarter than Einstein, and he is constantly looking after you day and night. You would know that you are very important.

If You Can Count to Four - 49

Now, how does one change his consciousness from a consciousness of inferiority to a consciousness of confidence in one's self. We must learn who we are and that we have an important role to play in the game of life.

We must realize that we are indispensable channels of service to humanity. That we have both a conscious mind in a subconscious mind and that we reason both deductively and inductively, which I choose to call the "A" type and "B" type of reasoning. The "A" type means that we can investigate before we accept it as true, the "B" type means that we can accept it on the assumption that it is true.

We must be aware that by virtue of the fact that our Creator created us with these marvelous faculties, he has a definite job for us to do.

This great life force surges through us 24 hours of every day. It is powerful. We have the ability to direct it into any design we choose. We can neglect to direct it and it is like a great river out of its channel. It tends to destroy everything in its course. But if it is harnessed, it can take electrical power to the millions. This great life force is even more powerful than the river when it is directed.

Down through the ages, men and women with vision and faith have directed this terrific force, and as a result, we have our modern way of life.

Recently it was my pleasure to visit Hoover Dam. Needless to say, I enjoyed the visit very much. But I marveled at the scope of its structure. The size and the color of the men who conceived it and believe din it enough to build it. Then, the great Colorado River, instead of wasting its mighty energies, was captured and used to supply water for starving acres, by the thousands, as well as to provide electrical power for Southern California. Also, Lake Mead, which is the largest man-made lake in the world, provides recreational facilities for thousands each season.

Did you ever sit in your car and wait for a train to pass? Did you ever let your imagination take you back to the time before the first railroad and listen in on one of the first board meetings where some men of vision and faith were trying to persuade the others that they could build a steel track all the way across the country?

If You Can Count to Four - 50

Can you imagine just how difficult it was to get the men, who lack the vision, to see how it would be possible, for 70 to 80 cars, weighing hundreds of tons, loaded with tons of freight, to travel across thousands of miles of terrain, through the cities, at perhaps 50 to 70 miles per hour? It took great faith and vision to develop our railroads. Today, there are men who have faith that in just a few years, we will be flying across the country in 3 to 4 hours in large transport planes.

Some believe that we will be communicating with each other without the aid of an electronic instrument in a few years. In other words, we will learn how to tune in on each other, at will, and talk to each other, without the aid of any device. Maybe so, maybe not, but it is no more fantastic than those who believed in television 20 years ago.

We could talk at length about the great (so-called) men and women of history who have practiced great faith but I am particularly interested in the millions of people who are suffering from misunderstanding of life and are not enjoying life because of a feeling of inferiority.

I want the housewife to know that she is filling the most important need in the world. I want her to know that she was designed to be a good wife and mother and that to be a good wife and mother is the greatest profession in the world.

I want to challenge every wife and mother in the world to assume a feeling of genuine importance and to know how needed they are. Fill our minds with the thoughts of who you really are and how important you are.

- The purpose of life is to live.
- To live is to express.
- To express is to be what you want to be and to do what you want to do and to have what you want to have.
- There is an abundance of everything you could desire in the universe.
- There are laws or rules of making available all the things you desire.
- So all you need to do is to learn the laws and decide what you desire, and then do something about it.

If You Can Count to Four - 51

It is your privilege to either say to yourself, "I don't believe all this" or to say. "I am open-minded and will assume that it is true until I prove it either true or untrue, inasmuch as it is good. If it proves untrue, fine, at least I exposed myself to the possibility of discovering that it was true. If it proves to be true, then I will always know how you feel happy, healthy and prosperous."

The indescribable abundance of the universe will be yours as you choose to express it, because now you know the truth about it.

Now you know who you are. You know that you are an important individual. You know that you have a special job to do in life. Now, you must neutralize all those false concepts of yourself; the idea that you were not as good as someone else; the idea that you were not as pretty as someone else, etc. The way that you do that is to assume the new premise that you are an exclusive, important individual and feel the new concept so strongly that your new concept becomes a deeper habit pattern in your subconscious than the old ones. Then you will automatically feel confident.

Confidence or faith is based upon knowledge of self. Your knowledge of self now does not justify feeling inferior. It justifies a feeling of real importance. You now know who you are and your relationship to your creator and your fellow men.

Now, you know that you can design your life. You can now decide the type of person you want to be. You can become a person of poise, charm, beauty and confidence.

You can have a beautiful home, car, clothes or anything you desire. You can have these through self-confidence which will make it possible for you to learn the rules of life. All these things come through natural means. You design all these things in the idea form, and then in due time, you will experience them actually.

Each idea has a season, just like each seed in the garden has a season. Do not get the idea that all you have to do is just think. All this is based upon natural laws.

The first thing one must do is to be able to think it in the form of an idea. Then the idea is the seed, which falls into the soil, which is the subconscious mind. The subconscious mind then tells us, from day to day, what form of action is required in

If You Can Count to Four - 52

order to bring about the fulfillment of our dreams. We will receive this daily instruction in the form of urges and feelings. *Our part is to respond, with confidence, and do whatever we are led to do.*

Sometimes it takes years to realize our dream and sometimes it takes almost no time at all. Suppose you decide you wanted to build a dam across the Mississippi River, just above New Orleans. You don't have the money, but you have the well-defined desire.

You start talking about it and pretty soon you begin to make progress, but it takes seven years before the dam is a reality and cars are using the dam as a bridge. But suppose that you want new clothes. You go downtown and buy them today. You can see that one case took seven years and another case took one day or less.

To gain self-confidence, may I suggest some things for you to do.

- Read this chapter, each night, before going to sleep for 50 nights.
- Attend as many lectures as you can on positive thinking.
- Obtain a recording on self-confidence and play it over and over and over as often as possible to yourself.
- Cultivate friends who have self-confidence.
- Associate, as much as possible, with people who have lots of confidence.
- Expose yourself to every possible source of information regarding the study of your mental processes.

You are an individual. You are exclusive. You are important. You are especially designed. You are no smaller or no larger than any other person in the world. You have a special job to do and enjoy and should not compare yourself with any other person in the world.

May I challenge you to dare to dream big dreams for yourself and your loved ones.

You can be anything you want to be and you can have anything you want to have.

If You Can Count to Four - 53

Make large plans for they have magic to stir men's blood.

6 - Money: What It Is, And How to Have Plenty of It

I am wondering if you would be happy if someone were to come to you and tell you that you could have all of the money that you desire to have. I am wondering if you would be interested in learning what money is and how you can have plenty of it. I would like to tell you what money is and how you can appropriate the laws, which will make it possible for you to have all the money you desire.

First of all, the majority of the people in the world do not have all of the money they need and desire, because they do not know what money is. Most everyone thinks that money is security, money is happiness and money is real. They do not realize that money is a symbol of something that is real and that money is not real within itself.

We have all heard that money is a medium of exchange. Exchange of what? There is something that is real and tangible and basic that money is the symbol of. Money is the medium of exchange of this thing which is real. So, first of all, I would like to tell you what money is, then I will tell you what money is not, then we will talk about how to have plenty of it.

We have said that money is a symbol and is not the real thing. We have said that money is the medium of exchange of something real.

- Money also is an expression of the real thing.
- Money makes it possible for us to express ourselves in life.
- Money makes it possible for us to do the things that bring happiness.
- Money makes it possible for us to have the things which are desirable.
- Money also is a container.
- Money is a warehouse, or a storage unit, which makes it possible for us to render the real thing, that which money is the symbol of, in abundance.

If You Can Count to Four - 55

- It makes it possible for us to render a service and money is a container into which we store units of service.

Many, many years ago, we did not have money. People, with their various abilities to serve, in the various capacities in life, for which they were especially designed, would render a service, then they would accumulate the results of that service in the form of barter.

Then, in their own crude way, they would exchange the values as best they could. That was not very convenient, so as men and women learn better how to exchange their services, they designed a symbol of the real value, which is service. They could store it up in the form of a medium of exchange.

Actually, money could be likened to a warehouse, thinking of each unit of service as so much value. Let's take an example of a man who earns $300 per month. This thing called money, which is represented by the term $300, is merely a method of evaluating the amount of service that man rendered in a given period of time. Now, if he consumes only $200 worth of service during the month, then he has $100 worth of service as a surplus, which he can store up in this thing called money.

In other words, he has $100 in a savings account. That is 100 little boxes into which he can store extra units of his service, which he rendered during the current month.

Now, let us assume that this man wants to purchase something which costs 1200 units of service. He lives on his 200 units of service, and he earns 300 units of service during the month, so he stores 100 units of service each month until he has his 1200 units in reserve. He has 1200 little boxes, each of them representing a certain amount of energy expended in the form of his skill. He can trade these 1200 little boxes for automobile or a down payment on a house or a refrigerator or whatever he desires.

That which he received, in the form of a house, automobile, vacation or whatever he desires, was so many units of service rendered by the people in other channels. He exchanged his accumulated service units for the results of the services of others.

You can see how money is not the real thing, but a medium or a symbol of the real thing, which is service. In other words, *money is in effect, not a cause.*

If You Can Count to Four - 56

People who think that having plenty of money would solve all of their problems are dealing with effect and not cause. The reason why the majority of people in this world do not have all of the money they need, is that they are dealing with effect only. They are constantly trying to harvest, which is effect, without planting, which is cause. If we harvest all the time without replanting, soon we will not have anything to harvest.

We have been talking about what money is. Now let's talk about what money isn't.

Money isn't service, money is the symbol of service.

The real thing is service. Every person was designed with the ability to serve, with a potential capacity to serve in an unlimited fashion. So, the real challenge is to get acquainted with the real thing, which is service, then learn how to render a quality and a quantity of service. The effect is automatic. Once we increase the quality and the quantity of cause, which is service, the quality and quantity of effect is automatic.

The way to have plenty of money is not to give our attention to money, which is the symbol, and not the real thing, but to switch our attention to cause, the real thing, and become an expert in the realm of cause, which is rendering a quality and quantity of service to humanity. So, the challenge is for us to switch our focal point of values and to change our habit patterns so that we become proficient and effective in the realm of cause, which is service.

As I said before, the majority of the people in the world do not enjoy an abundance of this thing called money because their premise of values has been false. Because they think that money is the real thing, they are seeking after the symbol instead of seeking after the real thing, which is service. So, the challenge for us is to find an opportunity to serve in an unlimited way.

We must be able to render a quality and quantity of service. Otherwise, we are not entitled to an abundance of the results of service. Of course, someone is going to say it is very easy to say, but what are you going to do if you had been thinking, all of your life, about the symbol, which is money, until the habit pattern is so deeply engraved, that you find yourself constantly thinking about money and are not particularly interested in service.

If You Can Count to Four - 57

The answer to that problem is to approach it scientifically, according to the laws of the mind. We have a conscious mind and a subconscious mind.

The *conscious* mind is that part of our mental processes, which is aware. The conscious mind is personal, and it is that part of us that makes it possible for us to imagine a brand-new idea.

The *subconscious* is that part of our mental processes, which is not aware. The subconscious mind is impersonal, and it is a storage house where we have stored all of our previous thought experiences in the form of habit patterns. The sum total of all of our thoughts in the subconscious mind is what determines how we feel and how we react to every situation at the present time.

Now, the technique of changing our focal point of attention, or our premise of values, is to decide with the conscious mind, where the will power is, and where the capacity to design a new idea exists. Let us appropriate this capacity, which we have, and let us design a new pattern, according to our desires.

Now that we are aware of the real thing, now that we are aware of our opportunities to find an opportunity to serve, it is our privilege to use our intelligence to find a particular channel of service which we enjoy so much we would be willing to serve in it without financial remuneration.

How many of you know of a certain thing that you would like to do regardless of whether you were paid for it or not? Do you suppose that if Ben Hogan never received another dollar for playing golf, he would quit playing golf? Do you believe that all of the great athletes, in the many phases of athletics, would quit playing their various games, if they found themselves, suddenly, in a position, where they were not going to be paid for their activities?

We all know that they enjoyed these games in the beginning and that is why they ultimately became professionals. In the beginning, they were attuned to the very nature of the activity. Every one of us is especially designed to serve in some particular capacity or channel of service to humanity. When we find it, we will enjoy it so much that we would do it without compensation if we could afford to.

When we realize this, we began to look for that particular channel. Of course, we will find it because of the very nature of our intelligence. The subconscious mind is connected with

If You Can Count to Four - 58

infinite intelligence, and through the proper direction of our attention in the conscious mind, we can direct the activities of the subconscious mind to find the answer to any problem to which we desire to find the answer.

The thing to do is to get a definitized concept of this basic premise. That the real thing in life is not money, but rendering a quality and a quantity of service to humanity, then habituate this concept by clamping it into place with our will power. Remember the will power story for it is basic and true.

The will power works just like clamps on some boards that have been glued together. While the glue is going through the process of drying, it does not have the power to hold the boards together, but the clamps hold the boards together until the glue dries, then the power of the glue comes in and holds it in place and the clamps can be taken off.

The will power, like the clamps, is especially designed to hold our attention to something new and desirable until the habit pattern is well established. We can then relax the will power and the habit pattern will take it over automatically. So, after the habit pattern is established on the new premise of values, we automatically give our attention to rendering a real service to humanity in abundance. This causes us to appropriate the law of sowing and reaping in the field of life, and money, which is the symbol of the real thing, begins to come into our storehouse in abundance.

Every person of historical importance became the type of person who would be written up in the history books, because they discovered this wonderful secret. They found an opportunity to render the type of service which they enjoyed. They learned to lose themselves in that service, until they forgot all about the financial remuneration. Because they were planting seed, in abundance, in the field of life, life began to pay off bountifully.

With your permission, I will refer to Henry Ford. You know that until the time he was nearly 40 years of age he had never amounted to anything from a financial point of view. However, something down deep inside of him caused him to spend all of his spare time developing the gasoline engine. In those days, only the rich people could buy automobiles. He believed that the common man should have a unit of transportation. He had an obsessional desire to design and manufacture that inexpensive unit transportation.

The story is a familiar one to every person in the world today. Henry Ford's objective was not to make a million dollars, but to render a great service to humanity, and because he found ways and means to render a quality and quantity of service to humanity, he became one of the richest men who ever lived.

Henry Kaiser is a modern-day example of a man who has looked for opportunities to serve humanity all of his life. Today, he is head of so many different industries, that I doubt if he is aware of all of them himself. By his very nature, he is constantly looking for opportunities to serve. We are all familiar with the record he made in ship building.

He also played a very important part in building Hoover Dam. If you ever have the opportunity to visit Hoover Dam, take advantage of that opportunity, and while you are enjoying being shown through that vast construction, think of the size and the color of the thinking of the people who first looked at this great chasm and saw the mighty Colorado roaring down into the valleys beyond. Think of the faith of the men who designed it and believed it was possible to build a dam across that mighty river.

Through the thinking of men like Henry Kaiser, this great structure was built and they were paid handsomely because they were dealing with the real thing. His attention was on rendering a quality and a quantity of service to humanity and, because of this, thousands and thousands of families today, in the valleys below, have plenty of water under control. Rich crops are being grown every season, and they have four or five growing season per year. They have no floods because the water is under control. Millions of kilowatt hours of electric power are generated as a byproduct of this great dam. There is an abundance of electric power and thousands of families every year enjoy sport fishing and recreational facilities in the largest man-made lake in the world, Lake Mead, because men dedicated themselves to rendering a quality and a quantity of service to humanity.

Of course, incidentally, they were compensated with millions of dollars for their services. I am sure that many of you are asking the question, "Well, how does this apply to poor little old me? I am just an ordinary housewife; I am just an ordinary insurance

If You Can Count to Four - 60

salesman; I am just an ordinary food supplement salesman; I am just a waitress or a service station attendant or a mechanic or a machinist. How does this principle apply to me?"

It applies to you as definitely as it does to Henry Kaiser or Henry Ford, because you have the privilege of switching your focal point of attention from your paycheck and to figure out ways and means as to how you can render a greater service to your employer and customers.

The challenge to each one of us is to realize that we have the capacity to serve effectively in some particular channel. And that we can become so effective in rendering a quality and quantity of service in that channel that we will reap a bountiful harvest, not only in the joy of service but also in the coin of the realm.

Now that we have discovered the law of sowing and reaping, which is appropriated by rendering a quality and a quantity of service to humanity, we have discovered the secret of life. Now, we can be anything that we want to be and we can have anything we want to have.

So may I suggest that you get a notebook and write down everything you want to be. You may think you want to be something that is going to take you years to accomplish. That is perfectly all right, write it down. You may want something that only takes a few days to accomplish, write it down.

Then, after you have written down everything that you want to be, on the other side, write down everything you want to have. List every category, your living quarters, your furnishings, your clothing, your transportation, the recreational facilities, like clubs, etc. several times each day, give some attention to this list, especially just before you turn out the light and go to sleep at night.

Then, you will find that you will begin to have a deep feeling regarding all of these things. Every day, on awakening, you will find ideas coming to you, from the subconscious, that will tell you what to do to make it possible for you to realize your objectives. Yes, it is possible for each one of us to design the type of life we want to live, and to design the type of things that we want to possess which will make it possible for us to express life abundantly. We have the ability to render the quality and the quantity of service to humanity which will make it possible

If You Can Count to Four - 61

<mark>for us to have the things that we want to have</mark>. Every desire has, within it, all of the intelligence and all of the wisdom and all of the ingredients necessary for its fulfillment.

Now let us briefly review:

- Money is a symbol, not the real thing.

- Money is a medium of exchange, which is the great convenience in our modern society. By the way, we never should feel negatively toward money, money is good.

- Money is an expression, or, money is that which makes it possible for us to express the type of life which we want to express.

- Money makes it possible for us to enjoy life by providing a means of exchanging our services for the services of others. When we are in and accumulate enough money, which is the symbol of service rendered, we can enjoy all of the finer things we desire.

- Money is a container, a warehouse, a storage unit, through which we can render more service in any given space of time than we need for our own expression. We can accumulate this service in the form of money, which is a container into which we can pour this additional service and use it later date.

- Money is an effect, not a cause, and so we do not put real value in money. We rather trust in our happiness and our security based upon our awareness of the real thing, which is cause, our ability to render a genuine, honest service to humanity.

- The great challenge is for us to learn how to render a real service to humanity. There are many unlimited opportunities to serve for every individual. Let us realize that we have been given, not only the privilege, but the capacity, to discover a great opportunity to serve humanity.

- Then let us burn all of our bridges and get into that particular channel for which we have been especially designed and let us become experts in that field so we

If You Can Count to Four - 62

can dedicate ourselves to rendering a quality and a quantity of service.

- We will be compensated in peace of mind and livingness, which is a continuous joy. That will be our first and most valuable compensation, but we will also be compensated in the form of financial remuneration in proportion to the quality and the quantity of the service we have rendered.

7 - How To Make Success Automatic

It is possible to make success automatic.

Basically, success is founded upon the type of thoughts which we permit ourselves to entertain from moment to moment. These thoughts are controlled by habit pattern. *Once this pattern is established and our thoughts become an automatic process based upon these patterns which we have developed because of our own desires, it is possible for us to establish sufficient success patterns in the subconscious mind so that we automatically think the proper thoughts that will make us say the right thing, do the right thing and will make us automatically successful.*

The majority of the people of the world are constantly thinking thoughts automatically as a result of habit patterns which they have developed because of the total of their past experiences. The result of the size and the quality of the thoughts they are thinking, because of this automatic mechanism, is causing them to not enjoy as large a measure of happiness, health and prosperity as they desire.

This is because the majority of the people are not aware of the fact that they are thinking beings and that they are thinking constantly and they are thinking one thought at a time. They are not aware of the fact that they can control this one thought, and they are not aware of the fact that they are what they are at the present time because of the type of thoughts they have permitted themselves to think.

They are not aware that they can be anything they want to be by learning to control these thoughts. This whole idea of being aware of the fact that we are thinking beings is not known by very many people.

Consequently, they have permitted themselves to think unlovely thoughts, limited thoughts, unhealthy thoughts, and they have stored in the abundance of these habit patterns, which are causing them to think their present thoughts, and consequently they are experiencing an inadequate expression of health, happiness and prosperity.

This great law, which I would like to refer to as the law of *cosmic habit force* or the law of habit, creates the whole universe. Every phase of expression in the entire universe

If You Can Count to Four - 64

operates according to this law of habit. Every phase of intelligence in the universe operates on the premise of the law of cosmic habit force.

This means that once a pattern is formed and is repeated enough time for it to become well established, it will automatically operate in that orbit of expression, unless it is consciously changed by a new decision upon it by the individual himself.

For example, it was my pleasure, a few years ago, to become personally acquainted with a man who had played basketball on one of the professional teams. I believe the name of the team was the Celtics. It was interesting for me to visit with him and to hear him tell of the long hours of training, in which he had to engage in order to develop the type of proficiency that was necessary in order to play on this great team.

He told me of the hours and hours each day that he would stand in a certain position, on the basketball court, and would turn and throw the ball into the basket. He did this many time and do it blindfolded and would almost never miss a basket. Consequently, after having developed a strong habit pattern so that his proficiency would be to a very fine point when he was engaged in a game, the play would seem to be automatic, and it was much easier for him to shoot the basket correctly than incorrectly.

Also, I saw a movie a few years ago that showed a man and his wife in a carnival act. The man would take swords or daggers and, from a distance of 10 or 15 feet, would throw them at his wife who was standing up against the wall. He would literally wrap his wife up with these daggers, throwing them and sticking them in the wall, just a fraction of an inch from her body.

As the story progressed, it showed that the wife had proved to be unfaithful to her husband and he became quite angry with her. So he decided to use one of these daggers in the show to kill her and instead of throwing it into the wall, just inches from her heart, he was going to throw it into her heart.

But, it portrays in the picture that, because he had been doing this so long, and had thrown these daggers so many thousands of times, he had developed such efficiency, based upon this law of habit, that he could not break that law. He could not cause

If You Can Count to Four - 65

the dagger to go into her heart. It would go, automatically, to the same spot where he had thrown it so many thousands of times before.

Isn't it interesting to know that we can design the type of life that we desire to live, that we can design the type of things that we desire to have and we can give our attention to these things so many times and control our attention and direct our attention on the assumption that we already are what we want to be and we already have what we want to have, until we automatically think these thoughts constantly, and by so doing, we appropriate the great law of appropriation of the great inexhaustible universe and can we realize our objectives automatically?

So the important thing for each of us to become particularly aware of is that there is such a law, and that this law is available for each one of us to use.

This is not a special privilege for just a certain few in the world, but because we are human beings and because we have a conscious mind and a subconscious mind and our thinking processes function according to an exact science, an exact set of rules and laws, just as tangible as electricity, chemistry, or mathematics and that these laws are available to us, we can learn to use them constantly, whether we are aware of it or not.

In fact, we must realize that at this moment we are a bundle of habits. Everything we do spontaneously, without giving our conscious attention to it, comes as a result of a habit pattern that is stored in the subconscious. We are so familiar with this law of habit, in certain respects, that we overlook its profound power and possibilities.

We overlook the fact that we can appropriate this simple law, and by appropriating it can direct our attention to it and control it and make it a habit. By so doing we can be the type of person that we want to be and have the things that we want to have.

Think how wonderful it would be to be able to be a person of poise and self- confidence, a person who feels comfortable in every situation in life, socially and in business and in all human relations, to have entertained a proper thoughts, so many times, under all of these various conditions, that we automatically react to every situation with love and kindness

If You Can Count to Four - 66

and humility, to be able to say the right thing at the right time, and think the right thoughts at the right time and do the right thing at the right time on every possible occasion. We can do those things by appropriating this wonderful law of habit.

Many years ago, before I understood this law as thoroughly as I do at the present time, I read an article in a magazine. The title of it was: "You can completely change your life in just 30 days." At the time my life certainly needed changing, and the title of that article appealed to me so I read it thoroughly. It had a very simple but profound message.

The lady who wrote the article merely said that if you were to decide, at the beginning of 30 days, the type of person that you would like to be, the type of life that you would like to be living, that by directing your thoughts on the assumption that you already were that type of person, in just 30 days, you would actually be that type of person.

Each day she gave some simple little suggestions regarding some exercises that would help to control one's attention. She suggested that we write down, in a notebook, in words which were meaningful to us, what we wanted to be, so that if anyone else would come along and read the note book, they would get a distinct mental picture of what we had in mind.

She suggested that we dramatize this new concept of ourselves by enacting little dramas with a close, trusted friend from the standpoint of our dream fulfilled. In other words, we would assume that we are already the type of person that we want to be and we would imagine some little event which could happen only if we have attained our objective. Then we should ask a trusted friend to help us dramatize this little event on the assumption that we had already attained our objectives.

She suggested that if we would do this it would recondition the old habit pattern and condition the new habit pattern in the subconscious until we would feel natural in the new concept of ourselves. Hence, within 30 days, we would have uprooted the old habit pattern, which was causing us to live in undesirable type of life and we would be living the desirable type of life which we have designed ourselves.

That was a very challenging article. I will remember it as long as I live. It has meant a great deal to me in the last 10 years.

If You Can Count to Four - 67

I am sure that everyone understands that a child, from the time it is born, all the way through its growing period, appropriates this law constantly. It is particularly true when it learns to walk. All of us have watched a child trying to take its first step.

The first thing that happens is that the child observes an adult walking, and it stirs within its heart a desire to imitate the adult. The child imagines itself walking like an adult. It attempts to take its first step, but, of course, there are no tracks in the subconscious, there are no patterns upon which the thought can travel, so the child stumbles and falls.

However, cost of a burning desire to learn how to walk it gets up and tries again and again in each effort establishes a little deeper track in his subconscious. Pretty soon, after many efforts, the child finds that he can walk all the way across the room and then begins to walk constantly, day after day, and soon he can walk all over the house. Soon walking is no longer a problem.

The average observer says it is just a habit. Actually, what happened is that a brand-new track was built in the subconscious mind. The average observer is not aware that the of the fact that he has just watched an example of one of the greatest principles in the whole universe, a principle which, once understood intimately and on a basis where the individual can appropriate it in his own individual life, will make it possible for him to design the type of life that he would like to live and by making every effort to be this type of person, over and over again, hundreds and hundreds of times, one day he will suddenly realize he actually is the person he dreamed that someday he would be.

As I said, everyone has a certain idea of the law of habit, but a majority of people take it for granted. I would like to describe this idea so effectively that you will thoroughly understand it and will be able to be the type of person you want to be and you can have the things you want to have, automatically.

Let's challenge ourselves to use this great principle to cause ourselves to be the ideal type of person. I am thinking now of the quality of kindness. Kindness is a quality of love. Even in the sacred writings it is recorded that love suffereth long and is kind.

If You Can Count to Four - 68

Love is kind. Each one of us who understands the law of love reacts kindly to every person and to every situation. Consider the difference in the individual who has appropriated this great law of habit so that he habitually and spontaneously responds to every situation with an attitude of extreme kindness.

Compare this person with the one who has unconsciously made it a habit to be unkind or to be critical or sarcastic or crude in any fashion. I am sure we can recognize the possibilities and the challenge of using this great law to become a habitually kind person instead of an unlovely person.

I am also thinking of the quality which is commonly referred to in the world today as positive thinking. Think what a tremendous challenge it is to make a habit to always entertain positive thoughts.

A positive thinking person is one who has made a habit of always seeing the good in every situation. I believe that when one is able to see the ultimate truth in every situation he will always see the good in it. One who has developed this habit of positive thinking always sees the beauty in every situation, and the true and the desirable. He always reacts, not only with kindness, but with enthusiasm and with a positive feeling of joy and peace and understanding.

On the other hand, it seems that many people in the world constantly react negatively to situations in life is a matter of habit. They see that which seems to be inadequate in each situation. They react critically and they have the attitude of fault finding as a matter of habit. They do not realize that what they see in any situation and in each person is not really the true situation. They are seeing what they are because they are seeing through their own experiences which are stored in the subconscious.

We do not see with the natural physical eye, it is only an instrument of the seer. The seer is the subconscious, which is our being. Solomon of old said that, "As a man thinketh in his heart," or the subconscious mind, "so is he." This means that he is what he is because of what he thinks in the subconscious mind, and I am what I am because of what I think and have stored as habit patterns in my subconscious mind and you are what you are because of the sum total of your habit patterns in the subconscious and whatever we are makes it possible for us to see what we see in every life situation.

If You Can Count to Four - 69

However, most people are still operating under the false illusion that they actually see what is in that situation, instead of knowing they see only what they are capable of seeing, based upon their experience and the habit patterns of their subconscious mind. It is a tremendous discovery to be able to use this great law of habit and to know that when we observe things on the outside of us, we see what we are instead of what really is.

Let's challenge our cells not to definitize the type of person we want to be. We want to be a kind person. We want to be a person of wisdom. We want to have the qualities humility, courage, faith, enthusiasm and the capacity to enjoy life as a matter of habit.

We want to see the good, the true and beautiful in life. We want to see the abundance in the universe and we want to express this abundance. In other words, we want to live an abundant life, in a large way, because there is an unlimited supply of everything in this universe, not only of wisdom, joy and peace, but also an abundance of the material things.

There is a law by which all of these wonderful things can be appropriated in this law operates on a thought pattern. We are thinking beings, and we can appropriate this law of beingness, and consequently, we can appropriate unlimited abundance. The only limit of our appreciation is our own concept of ourselves and our concept of our desires.

We are the designers of our own experience. Our thoughts do not recede into the past, they advance into our future and become our daily experiences as they arrive.

So let us realize that the law habit is not something that we should take for granted. It is something that we should appropriate.

Let me review very briefly.

- Decide exactly what you want to be and decide exactly the things you want to have.
- Definitize them by writing them down and go over them hundreds of times in your thought processes.
- Think about the things you want to be, and the things you want to have, until habit patterns are established, in

the subconscious, in the form of tracks upon which the thoughts can function.

- Then, when you feel natural in this new concept of what you want to be and what you want to have, it is yours.

This law habit is a challenge, and by the proper appropriation of it, you can be anything you want to be and you can have anything you want to have.

8 - How To Obtain The Missing Ingredients Necessary For Your Success

Every normally minded person desires to be successful. I suppose every individual has his own concept of what success means to him. However, my conception of success is to enjoy a large measure of happiness and a large measure of health and prosperity.

To have a balance in livingness. To have, not just a lot of money, but good health and an understanding of the laws of life so one can live harmoniously with himself, with his fellowmen, and with his Creator.

There are many people who seem to have all of the necessary elements which would make it possible for them to be successful. They have the know-how, they have the energy, they have the prestige, they have the capital, they had the ideas, the enthusiasm, the courage, the faith and the stick-to-it-iveness. And they are successful.

However, there are millions of people in the world today who secretly entertain the idea of doing great things, but they excuse their lack of attempt to do great things or failure to reach that great objective, which is buried deep within their inner mind, on the fact that they do not have the capital, they do not have sufficient education, they are unable to obtain the necessary skilled labor or they are missing the necessary elements of enthusiasm, faith or courage. Hence, they justify never attempting to start out toward their objectives.

I have good news for all of these wonderful people who deserve to be successful, yet feel that there are ingredients missing from the picture which cause them to fail to reach their objectives.

There is a principle which makes it possible for them to obtain all of the missing ingredients, regardless of what they may be. I call this principle "The Mastermind Principle." *The mastermind principle is a friendly alliance of two or more people working together toward a common objective.* Employment of this principle makes it possible for a person to enjoy the benefits of the background, the education, the energy and the influence of other people as though all of these qualities were his very own.

For example, the great steel king, Andrew Carnegie, confessed that he knew very little about the processing of steel in the marketing of steel. However, he was very familiar with this mastermind principle, and he was able to attract men who were experts in every field. Through the use of this mastermind principle, he was able to become one the world's leading industrialists because he was able to manufacture less expensive and better steel than anyone else in the industry.

Henry Ford used to this great principle in building the vast Ford Motor Company and all of its subsidiaries. Henry Ford, on one occasion in particular, bought a coal mine and paid several million dollars for even it even though he had never personally seen the coal mine. Someone asked him why he would invest several million dollars in a coal mine, which he had never seen. He replied that he didn't know very much about coal mines, but, he had a man on his staff, who was an expert in that field, and had sent that man to inspect the property. When that man recommended as a good investment, Henry Ford invested in the coal mine, sight unseen because of his trust in this member of his mastermind alliance.

In other words, it was possible for Mr. Ford to have the benefit of this man's skill and special training and energy and judgment without having to possess those qualities himself. It was not necessary for Mr. Ford to know all of the technicalities of coal and all the factors involved in using good judgment in buying a coal mine.

Yes, I know someone is going to say, "Sure, Mr. Ford could use this principle and Mr. Carnegie could use this principle, but how about the average man and woman? How can they use the mastermind principle?"

Let me say that this principle is impersonal and anybody can use it who understands it. It is very simple. All any person has to do is to have an intelligent objective. Know what you want, then add up all of the qualities and assets you have which are needed in attaining your objective.

Then make a list of all of the qualities and assets needed which you do not possess. It may be capital, it may be skilled labor, it may be influence and prestige, or the knowledge and energy of men and women of certain capacities. It may be a group of people who will help you to believe strongly in your objective so you can feel enthusiastic and courageous about it at all times.

All you have to do is to surround yourself with men and women who possess the right characteristics and who can make the contributions you need to reach your objective.

There are ways of compensating all the members of the alliance which will cause them to be motivated to want to work on your team to help you reach your great objective.

Being aware of the fact that there is a law of motion is very important. You cannot ask someone to serve on your mastermind alliance unless you realize that he must be compensated in some fashion.

It isn't always necessary to compensate people with money. Quite often your associates would consider it an honor to serve as a member of your mastermind alliance. People are just glad to help you. For example, if you are in the direct selling field, and you feel you are a little weak on approaches, form a mastermind alliance with someone who is an expert on this matter of approaches.

Then counsel with them frequently, get together with him and talk it over so you can observe how he makes his approach. Have frequent get-together's with this person who is an expert on approaches so you can build your awareness and learn from him.

In other words, make your weakest point your strongest point through a mastermind alliance with someone.

As I said before, there are many millions of people who are not working toward their objectives because they do not understand how to supply the missing ingredients which are so necessary for their success. There are millions of people who seem to have everything necessary to reach their objective except the necessary capital to get the idea started. This mastermind principle can help any person who needs capital, as well as any other help.

If you have an idea in which you believe very strongly, you will be able to convince someone who has the money you need to serve on your mastermind alliance. If you believe in it strongly, you can get him to believe in it strongly too, to the point where

If You Can Count to Four - 74

he will either furnish the money or he will help you to raise the money through some legitimate channel.

Many people fail to realize that capital is easily raised, if you have a basically good idea which will render a quality and quantity of service to humanity based upon integrity and know-how. I know of many cases and I'm sure there have been many other cases in history were capital has been raised and objectives have been realized through the establishment of an alliance.

It has been my privilege to use this principle a great deal, in the last 10 years. I think one of the greatest examples, in my own experience of using this principle, was the conception, the design and the development of a corporation which I had the privilege of founding. It is the result of utilizing the great principle that anyone can be successful if they will find a great human need, find the answer to that need, and take the answer to that need, in quality and quantity, to the greatest number of people.

I sought a great need. To find the answer to this need, I had to first consider the development of the best formula for the product. I was confronted with many problems. I was not an expert. I had very little capital. All I had was the idea and the awareness of the inner workings of this great mastermind principle.

Through the use of this mastermind principle, it was possible to obtain the services of a leading specialist in America. It was also possible to attract leading people in every phase, which was necessary to complete the picture so this wonderful company could be formed and operated on the high principle upon which it was founded. If it had not been for the inner understanding of this great mastermind principle, the product would never have been placed before the American people.

This principle applies not only in helping us reach our objectives in the business world, but also in many other phases of our livingness.

I think one of the greatest examples of this principle is the husband- and-wife who have a very noble objective of living a happy life together and raising their family.

They can work out their many, many objectives as a family by constantly working together upon this principle. Through this friendly alliance, they can talk things over, they can stimulate courage and faith and enthusiasm, at all times, and keep their family life on an even keel in a very harmonious, happy and abundant expression.

It is a great challenge for every husband and wife to become intimately acquainted with this mastermind principle so they can talk to each other frequently about their common objectives and clarify their ideas to generate a high degree of faith and courage and enthusiasm at all times.

Another great example of this principle is the board of directors set up in the various religious institutions. They may be called the board of elders and deacons in some churches. It doesn't matter a great deal, what the respective titles are as long as there are two or more individuals working harmoniously together in a friendly alliance toward a common objective.

The frequent meeting of a mastermind group generates a power which no one individual could ever generate alone. This mastermind principle makes it possible for ideas to come into our being, that would never be realized except through this principle, because two or more minds working together could be compared to putting two or more storage batteries together. They had a proportionately increased total amount of power, according to how many are attached together as compared to just one battery.

This mastermind principle helps us to have more power and a higher degree of intelligence. A greater degree of wisdom is exercised through a mastermind alliance.

The great challenge in considering this great principle is for us to definitize all of our objectives in life and to realize that regardless of how great or how large a scope our objectives may be, through the proper use of this principle, we can supply all of the necessary ingredients to reach every objective.

We need never be discouraged and say we cannot reach an objective because we do not have the capital or the know-how or the influence or the energy to do it, because through this principle we can obtain the capital, the services, the influence, the know-how and every other missing ingredient.

It is difficult to emphasize this principle sufficiently that I know that millions of people today are not even attempting to reach their objectives because they feel it is hopeless. Let me assure you that regardless of what the obstacle might be or what the missing ingredient might be, everything you need can be supplied to the mastermind principle.

Now that we have a clear concept of what this mastermind principle is and what it does, let us identify our objectives and learn to go through the rather simple process of using this principle. Let us write down on one side of a sheet of paper all of the assets and abilities we do not have, which we need to reach our objective.

Then, let us begin to form a mastermind alliance with people who are able to work with us and to help us supply the missing elements. This not only applies to large objectives, but it applies to what might seem to be the smaller things we desire from day-to-day. It may be that we would like to become more poised than we are. Do you know someone who has the poise you would like to have? Then get acquainted with that individual and ask him to help you gain the poise you desire. As you visit with this person, you will begin to learn all of the ingredients which go to make up a poised person.

If you are in the selling field and there is some phase of your activities that is not as effective as you would desire, get acquainted with people who seem to be experts in that particular phase and asked them to help you by serving on your mastermind committee.

Through this principle, you will be able to learn from them how you can be more effective. I am thinking of one part of the selling field in particular. Many people in the selling field have a false concept of values. In as much as many of them do not have a great deal of money themselves, they have the idea that everyone on whom they call does not have any money either. In other words, they judge their prospects by themselves.

It was my privilege to mastermind with a gentleman a number of years ago who changed my mind on this particular matter and it has helped me a great deal. Instead of assuming that my prospects did not have any money, I assumed that every one of my prospects had a great deal of money. I presented my proposition on that assumption, and I was surprised and amazed at how many of the prospects did have the money. I found, because of my thinking along these lines, I was thrown in touch with a higher level of prospects continually.

If You Can Count to Four - 77

I urge you to assume that every party upon whom you call has plenty of money. You will be surprised to find that this is the case. When you assume that everybody has the money to buy the things you sell, your problem as a salesperson is to know the merits of your product so well and to be able to describe them so effectively that you will make it irresistible to your prospect.

If you do a good job, they will want it with a burning desire. Hence, they will buy it because they cannot resist it. If they don't have the money at the moment, they will find some way to obtain it. Your concern is not whether they have the money, but, whether you are able to convey your message so effectively that you can make it irresistible to them.

Now, all of this involves proper use of this great mastermind principle, which is an impersonal principle, and which will make it possible for you to obtain your objectives. In this case, your objective would be to render a quality and a quantity of service to your prospect by making him want your product or service so badly that he will part with his money gladly, knowing he will receive value much higher than the value of the money which he paid you for your service.

If should be a husband or wife, and you are having difficulty in your family relations, might I suggest that you use this principle and form a friendly alliance with someone who can give you some expert counsel, relative to your problem.

This mastermind principle can be appropriated to help you solve any of your personal problems regardless of their nature.

Realize that there are experts in every field who will be happy to help you, provided you will ask them and then compensate them. You can compensate them either from the standpoint of your appreciation or from a standpoint of remuneration or something else that would be satisfactory and motivating to them.

We can be anything want to be and we can have anything we want to have through the use of this great principle. We can supply all of the missing ingredients which will make it possible for us to be very happy, very healthy and very prosperous.

By using this great principle we can obtain the skill, the influence, the background, the know- how, the energy of other people, as though they were our very own, and reach our most

If You Can Count to Four - 78

cherished objectives. So, *make large plans because they have magic to stir men's blood.*

Let us think largely, let us dream largely and let us appropriate this great principle, which is available to every individual.

Let us be aware of the fact that through this great principle, we can be anything we want to be and we can have anything we want to have.

9 - *The Power Which Makes All Desires Obtainable*

There is only one power in the entire universe, but there are many applications and expressions of this one power. One of the most important expressions of this one power is what we ordinarily refer to as will power. Through the proper understanding of will power one can obtain the fulfillment of any desire whatsoever.

Let me hasten to say in the beginning of this chapter, however, that will power is not creative and will power is not the most important power known to man, but will power directs the power which is creative.

May I refer to the fact again and again that everyone is especially designed to serve in a particular channel of service, and they are especially designed to serve effectively in that particular channel. Even though this is true, 98 people out of every 100 are not aware of what their particular channel is. 98 people out of every 100 do not know exactly what they want to be or what they want to have.

But, those who have made the decision, and have become aware of what they want to be and what they want to have, will be very happy indeed to learn how to use the will power, and its relationship to the creative power, through the proper use of the conscious and subconscious mind.

Now let us define and try to illustrate will power. For example, let's consider building the top of a beautiful table. Several boards are necessary. These boards are finished, and arranged so that they fit beautifully together. Then our master craftsman puts the glue on these boards and sticks them together. But the glue, until it dries, does not have the power to hold the boards together. What does the craftsman do to the board, from the time he puts the fresh glue on, until the glue dries, and they stick together by themselves?

Using wood clamps, he clamps the boards together solidly told the board in place until the glue dries and the power of the glue takes over. You will notice that the clamps have a mechanical clamping effect of holding these boards steadily in place. But, only for a short period of time do the clamps serve this indispensable purpose. As soon as the power in the glue takes over, the clamps can be removed because they have served their purpose.

The will power is like the clamps which hold the boards together, and the law of cosmic habit force or the great power of habit in the subconscious is like the glue. When we decide what we want to be, we used our will power or our mental clamps, and we force ourselves to think in terms of what we want to be for a long period of time until we can build a new habit pattern in the subconscious, so the habit pattern will take over and automatically Cause us to think in the pattern which we have chosen.

This is all very simple indeed. The majority of the people in the world are not aware of this simplicity or just exactly how they can intelligently direct the use of this tremendous power so they can learn to be what they want to be and have what they want to have.

Let us take a few very familiar examples of how this works. A young man gets out of high school and he decides he wants to be a doctor. He knows that in order to be a doctor he must go to school for, say 7 to 10 years. At the present time, having just graduated from high school, he is not a doctor. He is just a high school graduate. As a high school graduate, he has just completed certain basic requirements in order to receive his diploma from high school, and from the standpoint of thought processes, his mental processes are not so arranged so that anyone can safely say he is a doctor in any field.

But, through his will power the can direct his attention, day after day, month after month, year after year for a long period of years, to the study of all of the facts and things that pertain to his chosen field, until he build hundreds of habit patterns in the subconscious relative to being a doctor. Having controlled his attention through will power a sufficient length of time, on each item, until it becomes established and the glue takes over, throughout the remainder of his life, he automatically responds from those habit patterns of being a doctor instead of a high school graduate.

So, through the use of his will power, controlling his attention until these habit patterns are established, he becomes what he decided to be. Now, every mental process, which he experienced during his years of training to become a doctor, were experiences based upon these basic rules.

If You Can Count to Four - 81

You can readily see that all he had to do was to make a firm and deep convicted decision that he wanted to become a doctor, and then follow through in his training, by using his mind and controlling his attention units, exposing himself to all of this wonderful information and experience.

In so doing, he changed his being or his habit patterns, so he could no longer say that he was just a high school graduate, but that he was a PhD in his chosen field, able to serve in a special capacity.

The same process, which makes it possible for a young person to become a doctor in his chosen field, is the same process that a housewife uses in making a cake. She decides that she is going to make a certain type of cake and she uses her will power and she directs her attention to the making of that cake.

Now, if she only makes one take, by having to control her attention to consciously, by the use of will power, the cake would probably be very good, but not the best cake possible. But, if she will control her attention by the use of the will power, and make a cake every few days, within a period of weeks, she will build a pattern of efficiency and she no longer will have to use the will power.

She will be able to take the clamps off and let the habit pattern takeover and then she will be able to make a wonderful cake on every occasion. I am sure all of us now begin to realize that this simple law and simple process makes it possible for us to change all of our old habits into desirable habits so we can be anything we want to be and have anything we want to have.

Frequently, people tell me they just can't change their old habit patterns, and they can't entertain these new ideas and make them part of themselves. They know it is possible for others to be successful and other people to have the finer things in life, but they just don't understand how they can do these things themselves.

Let me emphasize this simple fact. Everyone has a will power. Everyone has a conscious mind. *Through the conscious and subconscious mind, we are able to design, according to our own specifications, the kind of life we want to live and the type of things we want to have.*

By designing these desires with our conscious mind and implanting them into our subconscious mind, which has access to unlimited resources of wisdom and knowledge, we will have all of the necessary ingredients to make our dreams come true. But, we must discipline ourselves and not continue to let the old habit patterns dominate us.

We all know that the most comfortable thing to do is to just sit back and relax and let the old habit patterns dominate our lives. We don't want to use any extra energy to think the thoughts or to entertain new ideas, new plans or any new activities. All we want to do is to let our thoughts run on the old tracks which have been established for years.

However, it is our privilege to decide exactly what we want to be an exactly what we want to have, and through the use of our will power and self-discipline, we can direct our attention toward these new things, and can neutralize all the old patterns and make new patterns so we automatically become want to be and want to have.

The average person could literally turn the world upside down and they would become keenly aware of this simple use of will power and self-discipline. Every great man, and every great woman, in history, discovered the use of the will power and self-discipline in order to become great in their particular channels of service.

They had to learn to say, "No, thank you" to everything with which they were confronted, from day to day, in the form of suggestions, which did not contribute toward reaching their definite major purpose.

I remember very distinctly how deeply impressed I was when I studied the life of Henry Ford. Henry Ford had many wonderful qualities, but one of the outstanding qualities was the fact that he learned to discipline is taught attention. He made up his mind that he was in the business of manufacturing and merchandising inexpensive units of transportation.

Hundreds of people approached him, trying to get him interested in other things because they knew he had plenty of money. But, Mr. Ford tells in his book under the title "my life and work" that he learned to distinguish between that which was relevant and material, and that which was irrelevant and immaterial and learned to listen only to that which contributed to his objective. He learned to say, "No, thank you."

If You Can Count to Four - 83

The majority of the people in the world are limiting themselves. They are suffering lacking limitation because they are victimized, every day, by suggestions and influences to which they should learn to say, "No, thank you, I don't have time. I'm sorry but I'm not interested in that because it does not contribute to my main channel of service to humanity."

This matter of using the will power and self-discipline not only applies to controlling our attention to help us to design that which we want to be and that which we want to have, but it also helps us to establish habit patterns, so we can refuse to let any outside force interfere with our giving our time and efforts and energies toward the reaching of our dreams and objectives.

We all know that happiness is a state of mind. We all know that a state of mind is developed because of the thoughts which we permit ourselves to think.

It takes quite a little will power and self-discipline to read the various publications and not be bothered by all of the tragedies and negative situations which are described and reported. I subscribe to a few select magazines and newspapers which I can, in a minimum of time, scan through the important developments in the news of the world from a positive point of interpretation.

Consequently, through the use of will power and self-discipline, I do not expose my subconscious from day to day to dozens of negative situations which are none of my business. Hence my time and energy are not wasted on something which does not contribute to the wonderful channel of service in which I happen to be engaged.

I would highly recommend that you take inventory of how much time you spend each day reading a newspaper. Find that portion of the newspaper, which seems to engage most of your attention and classify whether it is positive or negative.

Also, your television programs, the magazines which you read, and the people with whom you associate, could be classified into categories of positive or negative. Every category of contact with life should be classified and listed in two columns, one positive and one negative.

Through the use of will power, you can develop a new habit of giving attention only to that which is positive and not allowing negative situations to occupy your attention. This will be a little

If You Can Count to Four - 84

difficult, and it will take a little time to build these new thought patterns, but through the wonderful mechanism of habit and the instrument of the will power, you can begin now to direct your attention along any particular channel of thought which you desire.

You will have to clamp that attention unit hard at first, because it wants to run on the old undesirable pattern, but, after you have clamped it there, with the will power, for a period of time, a new track has been built and you can take the mental clamp off. Your thoughts will run automatically on the desired track and you will begin to experience a state of happiness and joy and livingness which you would have never been able to experience before because you are now free of all negativity. All of your thoughts, in the future, will automatically go along the lines of the good, the true and the beautiful.

At any given split second of our lives, there is enough of the sad and discouraging and the disappointing to them to demand all of our attention. Also, at the same split second, there is enough of the good and the true and the beautiful to occupy all of our attention.

Inasmuch as our great Creator created us with the privilege of choosing, at any given split second, that to which we should give our attention, we have the choice and the privilege and responsibility of directing our attention only toward that which is good and true and beautiful. Of course, once we learn to see the truth about any situation, we will be able to see the good, the true and the beautiful in every situation.

We have been told all of the great sacred writers of the ages, to judge not by appearances. In other words, we are not to judge a situation just from what we see with the natural eye, but we are taught to judge according to the truth about it, the inner truth, its premise and design and why it happened.

I am very proud to be able to say that there is no situation in my life, or in any other person's life, that if we knew the whole inner truth, we would be able to rejoice and be exceedingly glad. We would see that the inner design is based upon a purpose and a noble objective as a part of an integrating idea. It may be expressing itself, in many cases, in a disintegrating fashion, but if we could see the whole, we would see the integrating part as the center of attraction.

If You Can Count to Four - 85

What appears to be tragedy or discouragement is merely a rearrangement of the component parts of the integrating center. If we are capable of interpreting this rearrangement, the net result is always good, true and beautiful.

One of the passages from the sacred writings says, "Blessed are the pure in heart for they shall see God." God is good and the heart is what we see with our inner mind. So, blessed are the pure in the inner mind because they see what they are instead of what is. The only thing we can see with a pure inner mind is that which is pure and that which is good and true and beautiful.

So let us open up our minds in the spirit of the humility of a little child and let us grasp as much as possible of these great inner truths of the universe. Let's realize that we have a conscious mind which can reason either "A" type or "B" type and that we have a subconscious mind which is our connecting link with infinite intelligence.

Through the proper use of directing our attention in the conscious mind, we can establish any new habit pattern we desire. Through the proper use of will power and self-discipline, we can neutralize or eliminate or annihilate any old undesirable pattern and can replace it with any desirable experience choose.

We can, through the proper use of our mental powers, set the great universal law in motion, and we can become anything we want to be and we can have anything we want to have. We learned previously that we think only one thought at a time, we are thinking constantly, we can control that one thought, we are what we are right now because of the sum total of our thoughts throughout the past, and we can become anything we want to become by being keenly aware of this one thought.

Through the will power, we direct it so it expresses itself in regard to our dreams until it becomes a habit pattern, so we automatically think in terms of our dreams fulfilled.

So, let's definitize what we want to be.

- Do you want to be genuinely happy? Do you want to understand the inner laws of harmony, peace, joy and expression? You can be that kind of a person.

If You Can Count to Four - 86

- Do you want to be a person of wisdom to know how to apply the facts? You can be that kind of a person by appropriating these suggestions.

- Do you want to be a person of poise, have a beautiful soul filled with love, kindness, compassion, humility and understanding? You can be that kind of a person.

- Do you want to have a consciousness of abundance so that you have facilities for expressing life? You can have all those wonderful things.

You not only can have a wonderful home, and a wonderful automobile and all the things that go with that type of home life, but you can have all of the things that your heart desires, if you will learn these basic rules of the mental processes.

When I say, you can be anything you want to be and you can have anything you want to have, it is because we live in an inexhaustible universe, where there is an inexhaustible supply of every desirable state of beingness and every desirable thing you can imagine.

Let me challenge you to make large plans, for they have magic to stir men's blood.

10 - *The Power of your Imagination*

If I told you that, by the proper use of your imagination, you can be anything you want to be in and you can have anything you want to have, would you be ready to receive that as a basic truth? In my research, I determined that it was a basic truth. I feel that how I began to appropriate this truth will be of interest to you. I assumed that it was true. I then figured that if it were true, what would be the first thing I would want to attain in the material realm? Would it be a new automobile or a new home, new clothes or a new income?

During my consideration of this phase of my research, I found myself driving along Wilshire Boulevard in Los Angeles. I suddenly realized I was right in front of a mobile dealer's showroom, where was displayed one of the loveliest automobiles in the world.

I pulled over to the curb and parked in front of the showroom. I sat there and thought over this wonderful discovery. I realize that, through the imagination, I could assume that I already had what I wanted to have, and that by the power of assumption, the power of feeling as I would feel if I already had the automobile or whatever I desired, some wonderful power within me would bring it to pass.

So I sat there, and my older model automobile, in which I had an investment of only a few hundred dollars, and I looked into the window. I saw exactly the make of car that I thought was the most wonderful car in the world. It was priced at almost $8000.

I visited with my wife along this line. She reminded me that I had maintained that the only thing I needed to be concerned with was the use of my imagination, that imagination was sufficient, that I need not be consciously concerned about how to pay for it, that as soon as I got this wonderful feeling from assuming it was already mine, all of the other things in the realm of the so-called "practical" would fit into place and rearrange themselves so the purchasing of the automobile would be no problem.

So, my wife and I Masterminded together. We wondered whether we should dare to make this marvelous experiment. Finally, we decided to assume that we were going to purchase

If You Can Count to Four - 88

the automobile that evening. We went into the showroom and went through the whole routine of sitting in the car and imagining that it was ours. We talked to the salesman on the assumption that we were going to buy it. He became thrilled over the idea that he was going to make a sale. He filled out the papers completely on the assumption that he had made a sale to the point of my signature on the contract. Well, I'll never forget how close I came to buying this automobile that evening, even though when I walked down I was a million miles from buying it.

About two weeks later, I was down in the same territory of Los Angeles, and I went through the same routine. This time, however, I drove it for about an hour all around Los Angeles, getting the feel, using my imagination dynamically, assuming that it was already mine in every phase of feeling it. I came very close to purchasing the automobile that day, because in those two weeks something had happened in my business activity.

I found I had new zeal, new energy, new enthusiasm and new dreams, and I had increased the activity in my usual business almost enough during that two-week period to justify the purchasing of the automobile. Whereas, previously I had been unconsciously loafing too much. I didn't buy the automobile on that second visit, but an appointment was set up for the next day. I went in at 6:00 P.M. the next evening and by 7:30, I drove this brand-new $8000 automobile off the showroom floor and into another part of Los Angeles to attend a sales training meeting. It was the first new automobile in my life.

It was an amazing experience. I had proved to myself that through the use of the imagination, the subconscious provides all of the missing ingredients you need. From day to day, I have proved to myself that this wonderful imagination has indescribable power because, as we all know, the imagination is the ability, the mechanism and the instrument that makes it possible for us to assume a new idea or a new state of beingness. In other words, it is the ability of the mind to design and experience, in the form of an idea, something new, something different than we have ever experienced before.

Through the proper use of the imagination, any person on the face of the earth can immediately assume that he is the person he would like to be. He can also assume that he has what he would like to have. But we must dare to imagine these things.

If You Can Count to Four - 89

Otherwise, we do not appropriate the great law of creation, because the first step in creating anything is to plant a seed. Now we all understand how to plant the seed in the field or in the garden. We know if we plant a good seed in the garden, when harvest time arrives, we will have a harvest in the proportion to the quality and quantity of the seed planted, which we all understand.

But let us dwell a little on the subconscious mind. What is the seed of life? The seed of life, which must be planted in the soil of the subconscious mind, is a well-defined idea. A well-defined idea can only be experienced through the mechanism of the imagination. Let us think of the imagination as a very practical thing, something which we shall use constantly and intelligently.

Let us begin to design the type of ideas which we would like to experience. Once we have designed the type of life we would like to live, with all of the things in our lives we would like to possess, it is for us to assume that we already are the type of person we would want to be and that we already have the things we want to have.

Then we continually ask ourselves the questions, how would I feel, what would I say, what would I do, what types of clothes would I wear, what kind of a car would I drive, what would all of the things in my life be like if I already were the type of person that I want to be and if I already had all of the things I want to have? That is the technique of planting the seed in the soil of the subconscious mind.

I know that some skeptical person is going to ask, "Well, how do I get from where I am now to where I want to be merely by using my imagination?" That is very simple. What happens after the farmer plants the seed in the spring of the year, until this seed germinates and grows and expands and renders him a giant harvest? What happens in the soil? What takes place? Where does the increase come from? Out of the neighbor's crib? No, it comes out of the abundance of this great universe. We do not know what goes on in the soil of the vegetable world, we merely know when we plant the seed that this wonderful infinite power of the universe makes it grow and increase and we accept the harvest with gratitude.

And so it is when we plant in the soil of life or the subconscious. Our only conscious responsibility is to design the type of seed

If You Can Count to Four - 90

we want to plant into the subconscious in the form of good ideas. It was a tremendous discovery a number of years ago for me to learn that every idea has quality as well as quantity.

Every idea has design. It has form. It has color. In other words, everything we see in the outer world was first an idea in some designer's mind. But each of us has the ability, through this wonderful imagination, to design the size, color, form, quantity and the quality which we desire to experience later in the harvest.

Our only conscious responsibility is to design, in the form of an idea, the type of life that we want to live and the types of things we want to possess and experience. It is our responsibility to design them and to plant them in the soil of the subconscious.

By assuming that we already are what we want to be, and that we have what we want to have, this wonderful seed is planted in the soil, and in due season, the crops are harvested in this dimension as well as a vegetable dimension. And in ways which we know little about, this wonderful seed will germinate and grow and increase and become, in the outer world, exactly the same size and color and design as the idea contained. I don't know exactly, in detail, where you are going to get the money and how you can afford it and how all this is going to come to pass, but in a general sense, I know that you will get the money, you will get all the necessary ingredients which are indispensable in order for you to experience your dream fulfilled, as all the necessary ingredients provided which caused one grain of corn, having fallen into the soil to come up and grow into a large stalk with two or three large ears, with hundreds of grains on each ear.

Where did this little grain of corn get all of the additional material, the additional ingredients, the additional power to become a large stalk of corn with three large ears on it, with hundreds of additional grains equal or greater than itself? The great master teacher said, "We live by faith and not by sight."

Too many people in the world today have to see everything with the natural eye before they can believe it, yet we believe in the usual routine from spring until fall in the agricultural world. We believe that, in the animal world, there must be a time period before a little offspring can be born. We understand, in the human family, that it takes a period of time before a child can be conceived and then be born.

If You Can Count to Four - 91

We don't know how the increase comes exactly, but we know, by faith, that the power is there to fulfill every ingredient. It has been said, by great men of old, that every idea contained, within itself, all of the necessary ingredients for its fulfillment.

It has been my privilege to experiment with this great idea of the imagination, to test it out in the realm of things and in the realm of states of beingness. Let me assure you, from experience, that this great imagination works and scientifically as electricity or mathematics or chemistry. We can depend upon it. All we have to do is to use this wonderful imagination to dare to design and to dream the things we want to experience, the type of life we want to live, and in ways which we know very little about, our dreams will be fulfilled through the magic power of the infinite intelligence which we can contact with the proper use of the conscious and subconscious mind.

What do you want to be? What do you want to have? I'll continue to ask that question until you will dare to begin to use these wonderful principles. It always has amazed me that 98 people out of every 100 have not discovered how to use the imagination.

I know many hundreds of people who have attended lectures and read books by the hundreds and they still do not consciously use the imagination. They do not dare dream or assume that they are something which they are not at this moment. They do not realize that the subconscious mind does not know anything about the past or the future. It only knows about the present.

They do not realize that in order for them to become something which they are not at the present time, they must assume that they already are it. They must start acting as though they are already what they want to be. In other words, if you want to be truly successful, you must say constantly to yourself, "I am truly successful," not "I am going to be truly successful," because when you say you are going to be truly successful, you are confessing that you were not truly successful.

Then, the subconscious picks up the inference that you are not successful and brings that type of harvest into your life. But, dare to believe this principle and start saying to yourself that you are successful. *Say to yourself, "I am successful, I am happy, I am prosperous, I am poised, I am very healthy, I am*

If You Can Count to Four - 92

a person of wisdom, I am a person of peace and happiness and joy and gentleness and faith and meekness, I am a person of enthusiasm and conviction."

Put everything you want to be in the form of the present and start making statements to yourself and the attitude of ability and prayer. That is the way the subconscious will receive it and will bring it to pass, in due season, when you do not lose your faith. As long as you have this well-defined idea of what you want to be and have, you are practicing scientific faith. But, if you have an ounce of doubt in this principle, you will destroy the mental mold. You will destroy the design, and you will not experience, in perfection, that which you desire.

So, let me challenge you to study this great principle. Learn how to use the imagination. Practice using the imagination and dare to dream largely. It doesn't cost a penny to dream largely and since we live in an inexhaustible universe, there is no reason why we should dream limited dreams. It is just as easy for this great power to answer this principle when you appropriate it largely as it is when you appropriate it in a small way.

Let us make large plans, for they have magic to stir men's blood.

11 - How To Obtain An Increase In Income

Would you like to obtain a raise in your salary? If you are a salesperson working on commission, would you like to have an increase in your earnings? Certainly any person in his normal mind would say, "yes," to both of those questions. It is possible for you to obtain a raise in your salary, or if you are on a commission basis, an increase in your earnings, if you will learn a very simple principle was I choose to call the habit of going the second mile.

First, let me define what I mean by the habit of going the second mile. It means rendering more service than what is it usually expected and rendering that extra service in a spirit of joy or in a spirit of positiveness.

Fortunately, we are dealing with a basic law. A law which is as tangible as gravity, electricity or chemistry. This law deals with the mental processes, and it responds to our thoughts as tangibly as the soil causes the seeds to germinate, to grow, and in time, rendering a harvest.

Not in the spirit of criticism, but in the spirit of analysis, it seems that the majority of the people in the world are in the habit of rendering barely the amount of service which is necessary to meet the minimum requirements in order to receive their paychecks. *A few people in the world have developed the habit of rendering more service than what is expected of them. They appropriate the law of increasing returns. They sow generously, therefore, they reap generously.*

There are a number of reasons why it pays to develop this wonderful habit of going the second mile. I would like to enumerate a few of them. Rendering this additional service, more service than that which is usually expected, brings one to the favorable attention of those who can provide opportunities for a promotion. Needless to say, it is necessary for us to come to the favorable attention of those who are in a position to do us a favor or provide us additional opportunities. So, the one way for us to come to the favorable attention of those who can help us is to go the extra mile in service.

If You Can Count to Four - 94

For example, recently a friend of mine was telling me that he was quite favorably impressed by an outstanding young man who waited on him when he went into one of the larger service stations to buy a tank full of gasoline. This young man fill the tank, check the air in the tires, check the oil, then he went around and cleaned all of the glass on the car. Instead of giving it just a lick and a promise, he did a very thorough job in every part of his service. He seemed to have great joy in giving that extra attention. He did all of this in a wonderful spirit of helpfulness.

When my friend offered him a generous tip he refused to accept it, saying it was his pleasure to do this, that he enjoyed it very much. My friend told me that he was so deeply impressed with this young man that since that time he drops four or five miles out of his way to go into this particular service station to have his car serviced.

In other words, the attitude on the part of this young man working in the service station came to the attention of my friend, and he became a loyal customer because of the practicing of this principle. He has told the service station owner of this, so, the young man has come to the favorable attention of his employer who has the power of rewarding him.

Another advantage of practicing this principle of going the extra mile is that it tends to permit one to become indispensable in many different relationships. This enables one to command more than an average compensation. In other words, it is one of the few legitimate reasons why any individual can ask his employer for a raise in salary.

Another advantage of going the extra mile is that it protects one against the loss of employment and places them in a position to choose his own particular position in life and the conditions under which he will work. He can also expect new promotional opportunities.

It enables one to profit by the law contrast. The majority of people do not practice the habit of going the extra mile to try to get more than that to which they are entitled.

Making the extra mile principle part of one's habitual expression for all humanity leads to the development of a positive attitude, and habitually rendering more service than that which is usually expected, tends to change our basic habit patterns from a negative to a positive and, of course, one of the most desirable traits in the world is a positive mental attitude.

Practicing the habit of going the second mile, or rendering more service than that which is usually expected, tends to develop a keen alert imagination as it is a habit which keeps one continuously seeking new and more effective, efficient ways of rendering useful service. In other words, it creates a continuous challenge to find new ways of rendering a service because it switches ones focal point of attention from the "I" consciousness to the "YOU" consciousness.

It develops the important factor of personal initiative, without which no one may obtain any position above mediocrity, without which no one may acquire economic freedom.

Personal initiative is the most outstanding trait of a typical successful American citizen. It definitely serves to develop self-reliance. It serves also to build the confidence of others on one's integrity and ability. It needs one in breaking the destructive habit of procrastination, which is among the more common causes of failure in all walks of life.

It develops definiteness of purpose, without which no one can hope for success. It makes easier the mastery and the application of the mastermind principle through which personal power is attained. The mastermind principle is a system by which two or more individuals form a friendly alliance to work together toward a definite major purpose.

We get our cue to the soundness of the principle of going the extra mile from observing some of nature's ways. For example, nature goes second mile by producing enough of everything for her needs, together with an overage for emergencies and waste. Fruit on the trees, frogs in the pond, blooms from which the fruit is grown, fish in the seas.

Nature produces enough to ensure perpetuation of all species of every living thing and allowing for emergencies of every sort. Nature has arranged for all of her creatures to be adequately compensated by paying in advance for all they do in carrying out her plans. Bees are compensated with honey for their service pollenizing the flowers, but they have to perform service to get the honey and it must be performed in advance.

If You Can Count to Four - 96

Nature compensates the farmer after he has done his part in planting and tending his crops. It pays the farmer by yielding not only the original seeds he plants, but an over plus.

Throughout the universe, everything has been so arranged that nature's budget is balanced. Everything has its opposite, equivalent in something else. Positive and negative in every unit of energy. Day and night. Hot and cold. Success and failure.

Sweet and sour. Man and woman. Everywhere and in everything one may see the law of action and reaction in operation. The pendulum swings back the same distance that it swings forward. The same is true in human relationships and in the rendering of personal service as in all other things.

Put this down as an established fact. If you neglect to apply the principle of going the second mile you will never become personally successful and he will never become financially independent. This is borne out by the fact that all successful people follow this habit as an established part of their daily routine, in all their human relationships.

Test any successful person by this rule and you will be convinced. Observe any person who is not a success and you will be convinced.

One must render as much as he is being paid for in order to hold his job or to maintain his source of income, whatever it may be. One has the privilege of always rendering and over plus as a means of accumulating a reserve credit of goodwill, as a means of gaining higher pay and a better position. If no such over-plus is rendered, one has not a single argument in his favor by asking for a better position or increased pay.

Think this over for yourself and you will have the real answer to why it pays to render more service and better service than you are being paid for.

Every position provides one with an opportunity to apply this principle. This very freedom of opportunity is the major benefit of the great American system of free enterprise which has made this the richest in the freest nation on earth. It was to preserve this principle of free enterprise based upon the privilege of individual self- determination that our wars have been waged at such great expense.

If You Can Count to Four - 97

If you are a person who says, "I am not paid to do this or that, therefore, I will not do it," you are writing yourself an insurance policy against success. If you are a person who renders more service and better service than you are paid for and render it in a willing, positive mental attitude, then you are writing yourself an insurance policy against failure.

This basic rule of success has never failed to work and it never will. Lastly, remember that the personal attitude is the factor that determines, more than all else, the time that lapses between delivery of the service and the payoff.

I like the formula suggested by the great Napoleon Hill, which he calls the Q.Q.M.A. Formula. This means the quality of service rendered, plus quantity of service rendered, plus mental attitude in which it is rendered, determines the compensation one shall receive and the place one may occupy in the world.

The very famous, Knott's Berry Farm, near Buena Park, California is a wonderful example of the extra mile principle in action. We are all familiar with the story of how Mr. and Mrs. Knott, approximately 45 years ago, opened up a little roadside Berry stand and that by rendering additional services, more than that which was usually expected, the customers began to come in droves, so to speak, and they continued to increase week after week, until now Knott's Berry Farm has become an institution. They have continued to seek new avenues of increasing the amount of service, which they can render to their customers, in the form of good food and entertainment. They entertain you lavishly when your primary purpose of coming to their place is to eat a good chicken dinner. In just a relatively short while, they have grown from a roadside Berry stand to a multi-million dollar business.

Another famous example of this principle is the great Edwin C. Barnes, who rode into the hometown in which Thomas A. Edison lived, on a freight car just like a hobo. He walked into Mr. Edison's office and announced he had come to be Edison's partner. He started as custodian and he did such a wonderful job, even as a custodian, that he came to the favorable attention of Mr. Edison and went from one position to another until finally he became the partner of Thomas A. Edison.

Even the great Napoleon Hill served Andrew Carnegie for 20 years without direct compensation in organizing his great philosophy of individual achievement. His compensation has already amounted to the privilege of occupying a high place in the world and made many of his books bestsellers throughout the world. I highly recommend his books, "Think and Grow Rich," and "Master Key to Riches," to you. They have meant a great deal to me.

This idea, or principle, of rendering more service than that which is usually expected is closely associated with the idea of directing our attention toward something in particular and setting a definite goal. It also is an integral part of the development and functioning of the mastermind principle, the power which makes it possible for us to secure all the missing ingredients which are necessary for our success. It also ties in, very definitely, with the principle of self-discipline and the will power, as well as the principle of personal initiative and applied faith.

So, to be certain of securing a raise in salary, or an increase in income through commissions, switch your focal point of attention from, "How little can I do and still draw my paycheck and be satisfactory to my employer," to "How can I do more and get more efficient service, so I will become indispensable and valuable to my employer." Actually, the employer is not the one who pays your salary, you are. You pay your own salary. It doesn't cost your employer a penny to pay your salary, provided he is paying you what you're worth.

So, the only honest way that any employee can ask for a raise is after he has gone the second mile in quality and quantity of service, to the point where he is literally earning and producing more than his present income would indicate. Then, after he has produced this additional wealth, by rendering this extra quality and quantity of service, he is entitled to be compensated, financially, in the form of a raise in income.

Any honest employer will respond to this great principle automatically and will be happy to compensate accordingly, every employee who has rendered a greater quality and a greater quantity of service habitually than that which is usually expected.

So may I challenge you to analyze your own situation and to ask yourself continually, *"Am I just going the first mile or am I going the second mile in my relationship with my position and my employer?"*

If You Can Count to Four - 99

12 - The Power of your Emotions

When I was a youngster, down in the hills of Tennessee, a man visited our house one day and said he was going to put in a saw mill down the creek on our farm, so he could saw lumber for the people of the community who had surplus timber. I remember how excited I was the day they moved the saw mill in because it was pulled by a steam engine. This marvelous piece of machinery was so designed that, when the wood fire was burning at full capacity, it would turn the water into steam. It would then channel this steam into a cylinder, where it would move a piston, creating motive power.

This power would not only pull the steam engine and the saw mill along the road, but it would turn a large flywheel on which was attached a belt. This led to a pulley on which was a circular saw. Through the power created by this fire they were able to saw large logs in to lumber. All of that was a rather intriguing operation for a youngster 8 to 10 years old.

I remember how amazed I was that steam, compressed into a small chamber and directed where it would cause a small piston to move up and down, could create enough power to move this mighty steam engine. I remember they used just "snake" logs from the hills with this steam engine, and I was amazed at the power that it had in pulling these great logs. One morning, I went down to the mill early, before the crew arrived, and observed how cold this engine was and how powerless it was. I got up in the driver's seat and pulled all the levers, pushed all the brakes and clutches, turned everything, and nothing happened because the source of power was not present. The machine had not generated any steam.

The steam in this great big engine compares with the emotion in the human being. I learned a long time ago, before I understood the law of motion, that people around me who seemed to be very successful were those who had the capacity to feel strongly about life. They felt strongly about their business, in fact, they felt strongly about everything in which they were engaged. Thus, I have come to believe, that in order for anyone to be successful, they must develop the capacity to feel strongly about a great human need, and the capacity to feel strongly that they have the ability to take the answer to the need in quality and quantity.

If You Can Count to Four - 100

Every time we discuss any phase of success, relative to the human family, we must revert back to the study and a brief review of the conscious and the subconscious mind. Yes, the study of the conscious and the subconscious mind always enters into any consideration of personal success.

All thoughts originate in the conscious mind. The conscious mind is personal and selective. It has the power of choice. It is the male principle of the fourth dimension or the realm of mental action and reaction. The subconscious is impersonal and non- selective. It has unlimited power to take any order from the conscious mind and to bring it into fulfillment.

When we consider the power of the emotions or the power of feeling, we must become keenly aware of the intimate functions of the conscious and subconscious. The subconscious is impressed with every thought expressed by the conscious mind. It is impressed to the degree that the conscious expresses itself with feeling or a emotion, and every impression made with feeling or emotion, in the subconscious, must express itself outwardly in our environment.

Consequently, we must be very careful indeed regarding the types of thoughts, feelings and reactions we experience consciously. If we react with emotion or feeling to any negative situation in life, that impression will be made on the subconscious and then it must express itself in our lives.

That is the reason why we have so much frustration, unhappiness, in harmonies and trouble in the world today. The majority of the people in the world do not realize this relationship between the conscious and the subconscious mind and the importance of controlling their emotions.

Thus they have developed the habit of reacting to negative situations constantly.

Making these impressions in the subconscious is like the thorns and thistle seeds which come up in ones garden. Every thought is a seed. As it falls into the subconscious with a feeling, it germinates immediately and we must reap the harvests in our experience.

The challenge is for each one of us to become aware of the power of our emotions, and the fact that we can control our emotions, that we can experience only the desirable type of

If You Can Count to Four - 101

feelings, and that when we impresses the subconscious with desirable feelings, we can have only desirable experiences.

Previously, we discussed the importance of becoming aware of the fact that we are thinking beings and we're thinking constantly. All of our waking hours we are thinking consciously and all of our sleeping hours we are thinking subconsciously. The conscious mind is the father principle and has the capacity to design the type of lives that we would desire to experience.

It is through the conscious mind that we design what we want to be and what we want to have. The subconscious mind is the soil of life, or the female principle of the universe, into which must fall the seed of life. The seed will germinate and grow and become an outer experience for each of us.

Thus we must become aware of the fact that we are constantly sowing seeds in our waking moments, and we are constantly causing the seeds to germinate in our sleeping moments, and that everything we are at present time, every experience we experience as a matter of habit from day to day is the result of seeds we have sown with feeling sometime in the past.

We are the designers of the type of lives and the type of situations which we experience from day to day. There isn't anything on the outside of us in the form of climate, politics, friends or enemies, which causes us to be what we are today. If we are not satisfied with what we are at this time, if we are honest enough to admit that this basic principle is true, we will be able to see that we are in a position to do something about it.

All we have to do is define the type of situation we would like to experience and then began immediately to plant that kind of seed with feeling and emotion into our subconscious mind and make these impressions which will, according to the law as tangible as gravity, electricity or chemistry, develop into an experience.

If we desire to experience these desirable things as a matter of habit, we must entertain these thoughts until they become well-established and then the law of habit will come into play and, from that point on, we will experience them without any conscious effort.

I am thinking of a few examples of the power of the emotion. Did you ever wonder why some people can say a group of words and they will not receive even $100 a week for saying the lines, and a great actor or actress can say the same lines receive many thousands of dollars per week? The basic difference is in the depth of emotion, and in the control of emotion involved in saying the lines.

Did you ever wonder why one minister can give a message from the Bible and can hardly find a place to preach? They may pay him from $50-$75 per week for his services when he does preach, while another minister can give the same message and he is in demand all over the world and his income runs into the hundreds of dollars per week? This difference is in the depth of conviction, the feeling, the emotion, the expression, which all springs from an intensity of emotion well controlled.

Did you ever wonder why some sales people can say the same words, make the same approach, give the same presentation, give the same close, word for word, as another salesman and the prospect fails to react, while another person can come along and give that same approach, that same presentation, that same close and make many sales? *The difference is in the depth of emotion, feeling and conviction.*

Did you ever wonder why it was said of The Great Master, in the New Testament, that he spoke with authority and not as the Scribes? The Scribes were a group of people who were like a stenographer who transcribes exactly what is dictated. The Scribes did not do the thinking, but merely reported the thinking of others, and hence, they had not developed the capacity to express a depth of feeling in any of their experiences.

The Master Teacher, on the other hand, had a message in which he believed very strongly. With great conviction, he expressed it casually, but with the authority and with a feeling of knowingness. The multitudes followed him because of his great quality.

It is a great challenge for each person to learn to feel strongly about something. Unless one makes a decision and says within himself, "This I believe, with all of my being" he cannot express life effectively. Each person not only must find something that is good, true and beautiful, but which expresses itself with the depth of conviction. Each person must take inventory of all of his present habit patterns and gradually as they come up and try to express himself to neutralize them if they are negative and replace them with a positive track or habit pattern.

If You Can Count to Four - 103

One day, all the negative patterns will be eliminated or neutralized and all of his being will come from habit patterns which are positive and manifested in terms of the good, the true and the beautiful. Then, every thought, which comes from one's being will come with sincerity and with a depth of feeling. This great indescribable emotional power will express itself effectively and one's life will become a beautiful thing, a happy thing, a desirable thing.

So, realize that what we think consciously, with feeling, or with the emotion, is impressed upon the very sensitive plate of the subconscious and these thoughts must express themselves. *I challenge you to design good, true and beautiful ideas, and express them with the emotion.* They will be impressed upon your subconscious mind and immediately you will begin to realize good and true and beautiful experiences.

13 - How To Get Started On Your Dream

It has been said by a wise old sage, that to get started on a journey is to be half way there. Of course, it is quite obvious that if one never gets started toward an objective, it is absolutely impossible to ever reach that objective. It is of vital importance, therefore, for one to learn how to get started on ones dream.

Before we pursue the matter of how to get started on ones dream, let us review briefly some of the fundamentals which we have been considering.

What is the secret of genuine success? The secret is very simple.

All anyone has to do to enjoy a large measure of happiness, health and prosperity is to find a great human need, to find the answer to filling that need, burn all of his bridges behind him, and learn to take the answer to that need through a channel of service in quality and quantity.

It is very important also want to become aware of some of the very simple mental processes upon which success is based.

For instance, one must become aware that he is a thinking being.

The majority of the people of the world are unaware of this basic fact. Besides being aware that he is a thinking being, one must become aware that he thinks constantly and that he thinks only one thought at a time.

At times, it seems that one thinks more than one thought at a time because it is possible for us to switch our attention from one thing to another so rapidly that it seems like we're thinking of three or four thoughts at a time, but basically, and this has been scientifically proved, one thinks only one thought at a time.

Next, it is important that one become keenly aware that he can control the one thought which he thinks at a time through will power.

He must be aware that nothing on the outside of himself has any power to control him unless he permits it. This establishes the seat of control within himself.

If You Can Count to Four - 105

Next, it is important that he become keenly aware that he is, that everyone is what they are, because of the quality and the quantity of their past thoughts and experiences.

This basic truth is crystallized in the saying of wise old Solomon, "As a man thinketh in his heart, so is he."

Now, if we are thinking being, if we think constantly, if we think only one thought at a time, if we can control our thoughts, if we are what we are because of what we have permitted ourselves to think throughout the entire past, then, in order to be anything we want to be and to have anything we want to have, we can exercise the privilege of control over our thoughts, and from this moment forward, direct all of our attention toward that which we want to be and have. It is obvious that the law of cause and effect will bring about the fulfillment of our dream.

It is important for us to choose our objectives or our goals.

Due to the peculiar nature of the mental processes, operating through the conscious mind and the subconscious mind, it is necessary to choose or definitize our thinking relative to an objective or a goal. Otherwise, thought concentration to the point of action toward our objective or goal is impossible. It is amazing to me that only 2 people out of 100, according to statistics, have made a definite decision relative to their goal in life.

In order for one to be happy, healthy and prosperous, one must have an objective.

If he does not, he will not be appropriating the great power within himself.

It is important that one develop self-confidence.

One must feel strongly that he is capable of doing the things which are necessary to reach his objective. The basic cause for a feeling of inferiority is that we're making false comparisons constantly. We are inclined to compare ourselves with other people. There is really no basis for comparison between one person and another, because every person is an individual.

Everyone is especially and exclusively designed to do something well and possibly better than anyone else. Therefore, due to the fact that no two individuals are like or are designed for the same purpose, there is no intelligent basis for comparison of one individual with another.

- Realize that you are important.
- Realize that you are designed especially to do a great service to humanity and that you are different.
- Realize that you are exclusive.
- Realize that you have your own individuality.
- Become keenly aware of your individuality, and your great purpose, and then dedicate yourself to fulfilling that great purpose, and you will develop self-confidence.

In order to get started on our dream, we need to know the proper concept of money, which is the medium of exchange used in our economic world today.

Money is a symbol of service. Money is deferred service. Money isn't affected, service is cause.

So, when we get into the habit of giving most of our attention to the effect or a symbol, which is money, then we do not have very much money. However, when we learn to render a quality and a quantity of service to humanity, which is cause, like planting in the field of life, we know that we are compensated in proportion to the quality and quantity of service rendered, not only in the realm of joy and living, but in the realm of the finances as well. We will then have the proper concept of money and money will not be a power over us but we will be the power over money.

There is a great law in this universe, the law of habit.

It is sometimes referred to as the law of cosmic habit force. It is a basic universal law, which maintains that when we have a thought experience or a physical experience, which occurs over and over and over, it becomes established, and soon we think the thought or do the act. Therefore, we can learn to think, automatically or habitually, the thoughts which will cause us to be successful and we can learn to do the things, automatically or habitually, which will cause us to be successful.

There is a way for every individual to obtain the missing ingredients he needs in order to reach his dream or objective. I refer to the Mastermind Principle.

If You Can Count to Four - 107

Through this mastermind principle, which means the friendly alliance of two or more people working toward a common objective, one can obtain every necessary ingredient, the experience, the skill, the prestige, the time, the energy and even the money which is necessary to reach an objective.

Discovering this great principle and learning how to use it, will eliminate all need for an excuse for not reaching any objective in life.

Consider, too, the will power, which every individual possesses.

This will power is not the creative power within ourselves, but it is the power to direct our attention and to control our attention, at any time we choose, toward that which we desire to be or desire to have.

Once we used this will power for a brief period of time, controlling our attentions and our thought processes along constructive and desirable lines, the power of habit takes over and becomes established, and then we automatically do the things or say the things and think the things which make it possible for us to reach our objectives.

Another very important factor in getting started on your dream and having the dream fulfilled is to become thoroughly acquainted with the marvelous imagination which every individual possesses.

It is the instrument or the faculty to design and experience a new idea. Our ability to definitize a new idea, is like planting the seed of life in the soil of life. When we imagine and definitize an idea and plant it in the subconscious, the great law of sowing and reaping will cause the idea to grow and become a reality.

So, accept the challenge to constantly learn to use this wonderful ability to imagine. It is an ability which gives us the power to us so that we already are what we want to be and that we already have what we want to have. It is the power which makes all desires obtainable.

The habit of going the second mile is one of the most important principles of success.

It is unfortunate, but the majority of people in the world today are not in the habit of going the second mile. Going the second

If You Can Count to Four - 108

mile means rendering more service than that which is usually expected in any situation and rendering that extra service with a positive attitude. Every great individual in history discovered this principle and made it a habit. They always looked for an opportunity to do more than that which was usually expected and perform that extra service with a positive mental attitude. One of the finest ways in the world for you to realize your dream fulfilled is to acquire this marvelous habit of going the second mile.

It is vitally important that one learn the power of the emotion or the power of feeling, because when the conscious mind uses the imagination, and definitizes an idea, that idea must be felt.

One must feel strongly about an idea, otherwise it will not be impressed upon the subconscious and consequently it will not express itself in one's experience. So, if one believes in an idea of which he is designing with his imagination, the degree of belief and the degree of feeling determines the degree of power with which the subconscious will accept and express it in experience. Therefore, learn to feel strongly about the great need which you are trying to fill! Feel strongly about the answer to that need! Feel strongly that you are the one to take the answer to the need to humanity in quality and quantity.

Another important factor in attaining health, happiness and success, is constantly having peace of mind.

Harmony of soul. To have peace of mind, one must have a true concept of life, a true concept of the universe in which we live, a true concept of our relationship to ourselves and to our fellow men and to our Creator. There is just one great power in this universe, and it expresses itself at many levels of intelligence.

- The lowest level is the mineral world.
- The next level upward, or the second level, is the vegetable world.
- The third level is the animal world.
- The fourth level is where the human can express themselves through thought.

Thought with freedom of choice and decision. When we realize that this one power is within us, and realize that we have legislative and judicial and executive powers within ourselves, we know that we can refuse to react negatively to any life

If You Can Count to Four - 109

situation. We can choose to see the good, the true and the beautiful at all times. To know and firmly believe that all is good at all times, causes us to become invulnerable to in harmony or frustration, and we can always maintain a peaceful state of mind.

Now, give serious consideration of *"How to Get Started on Your Dream."*

First, take inventory of your present situation, relative to the size and quality of your thinking. May I suggest that you obtain a notebook and write down an inventory of your present situation, fourth dimensionally and third of dimensionally. You may wonder how to take inventory fourth dimensionally. Write down, in your notebook, your concept of how much poise, how much charm, how much kindness, how much love, how much faith, how much gentleness, how much patience, how many good qualities which are desirable, and how many bad qualities which are undesirable you possess as a matter of habitual experience at the present time.

That will be your fourth dimensional inventory. Be frank with yourself. If you feel that you are unlovely to any degree, write it down. By the same token, if you feel that you are to a large degree a lovely person, write that down also. Be honest with yourself in this inventory.

Now, write down your third dimensional inventory. Your third dimensional inventory includes the type of house you live in, the type of car you drive, the type of clothes you wear, the type of income you habitually receive. Everything you have in your physical environment is in your third dimensional inventory. Get a clean-cut, distinct picture of your NOW, fourth dimensionally and third dimensionally. That is number one.

Then, turn the page in your notebook and write down what you would like to be fourth dimensionally. How lovely you would like to be, how charming you would like to be, how much confidence, how much faith, how much patience, how much love, how much joy, how much peace, how much gentleness, how much kindness you would like to experience habitually.

Describe it distinctly, and definitize it in words, so you will get a clean-cut mental concept of what you want to be fourth dimensionally. Make quite a study of this. If you can't find any

If You Can Count to Four - 110

pictures, color pictures preferably, in magazines or newspapers, which seem to represent the kind of person you would like to be, clip those pictures out and paste them in your notebook.

Then, take inventory of the type of person you would like to be from the standpoint of the third dimension. What kind of house would you like to live in, what kind of a car would you really like to drive, what kind of clothes would you like to wear, what kind of a neighborhood would you like to live in, what kind of a country club would you like to join, what kind of friends would you like to socialize with, how much money would you like to have as a stable, basic income?

All of those things are your third dimensional desires. Write those down and definitize them in every way possible. Anything that you can do to cause you to become more keenly aware of what you want to be and what you want to have is very important in this regard.

Number three, have a little talk with yourself. You are constantly carrying on a conversation with yourself, within yourself.

Now, start talking from the position of your dreams fulfilled. Read the things you want to be and have, listed in your notebook, each night before you go to bed. Assume, through this wonderful power of your imagination, that you already are or what you want to be and you already have what you want to have.

Live in your dreams fulfilled as often as possible. It will take a little time for you to feel natural, emotionally, in your dream fulfilled, because each day, you must go about your usual life and usual work.

As soon as you learn to feel natural in your dream fulfilled, thinking from the position that you already are what you want to be and that you already have what you want to have, you will find that you have attained this new level of experience and you will be casually living in your dream fulfilled.

Actually, you will have detached yourself from the old inventory and will be making new inventories in your notebook. As you attain an objective, you will make up your new inventory fourth dimensionally and third dimensionally. You will fill out a new seat, with new objectives, new dreams and you will continue to do it time and time again. There is no

If You Can Count to Four - 111

end to the possibility of growth and expression. We continue to grow and expand and experience new dreams throughout our lives.

The way to get started on your dreams now, is to definitize them now. When you have attained the new level of your present dream fulfilled, you will be able to see further over the horizon of life and will be in a position to design a new dream of being and having. In turn, when you reach the attainment of new dreams fulfilled again and again you will be at a new vantage point and will live in a continually increasing abundance of living through all of your life. Isn't it a joyful thought to know that there is no end to the attainment of our dreams?

So I close with this wonderful challenge, **"Make large plans for they have magic to stir men's blood."**

14 - The Four Greatest Values In Life

To me, there are four values in life which stand out above all others. They are as follows: **Integrity, Faith, Courage and Humility**. Let us consider, first of all, Integrity.

Of all the values in the universe, to me, **integrity** is the greatest. This universe operates on the premise of law and principle. It is designed to operate basically according to an exact science. There is a variable quality and an invariable quality. There is an area of law which is inflexible and there is an area of flexibility, or personality, which is flexible.

But, integrity is a law, just like electricity, gravity, mathematics and chemistry. Integrity, when you thoroughly understand its nature, is something that one would not violate any more than one would violate the laws of electricity if one knew the consequences of such violation. I know that it is necessary to think of integrity as a moral problem until an individual becomes aware of the deeper laws underlying integrity.

In order to protect the individual from the uncomfortable consequences of violating the basic law of integrity, it is necessary that we approach this matter of integrity from a standpoint of morality. In other words, we must lay down certain rules and we must say that it is good if we observe the rules, and it is evil to violate the rules. And then, from a sense of fear, from a sense of respect and a responsibility, an individual, who does not understand the scientific nature of responsibility, will observe the law of respect or the moral aspect of the matter.

But let us all become keenly aware that integrity is a scientific matter, as well as a moral matter, and that when we know the truth about any situation, we will know the quality of integrity, and we will observe that law and that law will respond by bringing us harmony, peace and abundance.

I think the supreme challenge of the age is for mankind to learn that integrity is the greatest value on the highest priority list in the entire universe. There is no value in this entire universe. That should be as great in our concepts as integrity. To understand the truth about a matter is to act in truth, but not to understand it is to express ourselves, according to our degree of understanding, and it will react to us according to our understanding of it. This is a scientific matter.

Next to integrity, I believe that **faith** is the highest value in life. The English word for faith is an attempt to describe a mental function known to me as an inner understanding or an inner perception. The ability to see the invisible laws of the universe and to see how they function and to understand how they operate and deal with them in a tangible fashion while they are going through the invisible process and before they become visible. That mental quality we call faith.

When we understand the great underlying laws, the invisible laws of the universe, and we deal with them as though they are as tangible as mathematics, then we expressed faith. That is what we call faith. Since these great laws are infinite, and we deal with them in a relative sense, and the relative, in regard to the absolute, has size, color, quality and quantity, and we express this size and color, and the quality and quantity according to our faith or the size and color of our ideals.

In other words, our mind expresses through the instruments of our thoughts and our thoughts are contained in our words, which have size and color, design and texture. For when we say, "According to our faith it is done unto us," we are saying, "According to our inner perception and according to the size and color of our ideas relative to the infinite, it is done unto us." So faith is also a tangible law and not something that we just profess to blindly.

However, if we express blind faith and conviction in something and it happens to be, according to its nature or truth, it will also respond to us and bring us harmony and peace, but the challenge is for us to understand these things, and to study them so that we will foresee it and feel it with the inner eyes of faith! We will then be relaxed, harmonious and peaceful and express this life abundantly according to our own perception or our faith.

The next great value, to me, is **courage**. Courage is a function of mind that expresses itself in terms of intensity of attitude. Our ability to stand up and face life without fear. It really is a quality that is based upon our understanding, because our courage would depend upon our understanding, and according to our understanding, we will be able to react to life positively or with courage. We will be able to do the thing we fear in the process of gaining our understanding.

I think courage is that quality that would cause us to do the thing we fear, would cause us to run the risk of suffering discomfort, in order to learn how to live in a new area of understanding. If we do not have courage, we are afraid to learn new lessons, to accept new ideas and to have new experiences, to enter into the unknown in order that we might learn the unknown and make it known.

It takes courage to run the risk of being insulted in order to learn how to deal with a situation so effectively that we would not be insulted in the future.

It takes courage to jump off a high diving board for the first time when we do not understand exactly how to do it and run the risk of burning blisters on our bodies.

It takes courage to step onto a stage and make a speech and run the risk of being embarrassed until we learn to feel comfortable when making a speech.

It takes courage to punch a doorbell and run the risk of being met with unkindness or discourtesy at the door, or having it slammed in our faces in the process of learning how we may approach on the reference-lead plan.

It takes courage to accept a new idea on the assumption that it is true, and run the risk of having temporary failure and embarrassment if it does not prove to be true, in order that we might learn to get closer to the truth. Yes, courage is a great quality.

Courage is an indispensable quality and to me it is one of the four greatest qualities in the universe.

The next quality, to me, is the great quality of **humility**. Humility is that quality that comes from knowing who we are, in relationship to ourselves and our fellow man, and in relationship to the Creator of the universe and all of life. We know that of ourselves, we amount to nothing, but we know that when we are aware of this great power in the universe, that through this power, and the laws and the truth of the great appropriation of this power, we can do anything we desire to do, and we can be anything we want to be and have anything we want to have, but I think it is all in giving credit where credit is due.

Yes, humility is knowing the truth about our relationship to life, giving credit where credit is due. It is not the pollyanna-sissy type of attitude or the act that many people put on and call humility. It is a tenacious, stable type of thinking that comes from a habit pattern based on the understanding of life.

Do not think that we, of ourselves, in a separated sense, can do anything. We know that we are all dependent upon each other, upon our Creator, upon so many things. We must recognize that and give credit where credit is due and be humble and kind and we know that we will be harmonious and happy and prosperous.

And so,

- **Integrity** is the greatest quality in the universe, and it is a scientific thing. To know the truth is to have integrity. When you understand integrity you would rather give someone $10 than to beat them out of a dollar. You know that the law will bring you happiness, health and abundance if you practice integrity.

- **Faith** is that size and color of one's convictions and inner understanding; and the amount and the quality that one is able to express proportionate to one's individuality.

- **Courage** is that quality which makes it possible for us to learn new things and face the things we fear in order that we might continue to grow in our understanding of life.

- **Humility** is understanding our true relationship to life, and not to feel that we can do anything of ourselves, but we can do all things through the great powers with which we are one.

"Make no small plans for they have no magic to stir men's blood."

15 - How To Get A Feeling

It has been said by lettered men for centuries, and that to have a feeling of happiness is to be happy and have a feeling of abundance is to have an abundance, and to have a feeling of health is to be healthy.

At first, I did not understand the meaning of such statements, and perhaps, you will not, at first, understand the meaning. Now I do have some degree of understanding of such statements, and I find that they have scientific premises, based upon laws that are real and tangible as any other science of which we are so familiar, such as electricity, gravity, mathematics and chemistry.

The conscious mind originates a concept and expresses it in the form of thoughts, ideas and in the form of words. It has been discovered, in psychological research, that the degree of feeling put into these concepts, and expressed, with feeling, in words, to the subconscious, determines the action in the subconscious. That any idea, expressed with feeling to the subconscious by the conscious, must express itself as an experience. That is a scientific, proven fact in psychology.

Yes, any idea that is conceived and well defined, and expressed with strong feeling, is felt by the subconscious, and must expressed as an experience. And everything that is impressed upon the subconscious, by an expressed feeling consciously, must become an experience. Well, what do people want more than anything else? They want a certain type of experience. They want to experience a larger measure of happiness.

They want to experience a larger measure of health and, of course, a large measure of prosperity. So, we design our ideas to contain the type of experiences we want to experience, then we express them with feeling, consciously, and they are impressed upon the subconscious mind, which is the soil of life, and then, in time, when they have had time to gestate and to become an experience, we have the experience.

Now that is the general premise that can be pooled in each of our lives, but how do we get this feeling? Someone says, "Well, I have the concept, I would like to have a certain type of experience, but it does not happen in my life. What is the missing link?

If You Can Count to Four - 117

What do I lack? What am I failing to do?" The answer to that is you do not have the feeling for it. We must not only have a concept we must have a feeling for it. Now how do we get this feeling? If we can get the feeling, we can have the experience, no more second if we cannot get the feeling, we cannot have the experience, so the purpose of this chapter is to talk about how to get the feeling.

Now, I would like to introduce what I call the *law of reversibility*, which is a law in this universe, the same as any other great law, like electricity. The law of reversibility could be illustrated as follows: if you start with a dynamo and a crank on a wheel, you can turn the crank and the wheel and turn the dynamo which we will refer to as physical action. We can start with physical action, and by using physical action, we can turn the dynamo physically and we can create electricity.

On the other hand, we can reverse the process. We can start with electricity, and with electricity, we can turn a wheel or a physical action. In other words, we can reverse the process, we can start with physical action to create electricity or we can start with electricity and create physical action. I'm sure that everybody can understand that.

Now, let's apply it in a higher level of values. *We can start with physical action and create a feeling and then in turn, feeling will create a physical action.* Show me a man that has no feeling and if we can ask him to do certain things, which would be physical action, the doing of these things would create action which would be physical action.

Then we can cause him to feel a certain way after he goes through these physical exercises. We can create any kind of a feeling we want by getting him to assume this activity physically. To have him play a certain role physically, he will create within himself a feeling of that role. When he starts the action, he has no feeling for it at all. It is merely an exercise, a physical exercise.

Show me a man who has a certain feeling for a role and he will play the role and do the things that the role calls for. In other words, we can start with physical action and creating feeling, or we can start with feeling and create an action. That is the law of reversibility, and this law works on every level of life. On the first dimension, the second dimension, the third dimension and the fourth dimension.

If You Can Count to Four - 118

So, how do we get a feeling?

No matter how cold we may feel toward some idea, we identify the physical action in which we would exercise if we were playing the role, then we decide to do that, at first without feeling, then we do it over and over and over again until we create the feeling, and as soon as we create a strong feeling we are appropriating the basic essence of life.

We can consciously express this feeling; it will be impressed upon the subconscious and anything that is impressed upon the subconscious must become a habitual experience in our lives.

So, while education is a wonderful thing, it is not necessary to have a so-called academic education, perchance you don't have one. If you have one it is wonderful and I congratulate you, but I do not want anyone who does not have a so-called academic education to say, "Well, this can't happen to me," because it isn't necessary to have an education to propagate this law of reversibility. If you can act like a king, if you can feel like a king, you can be a king. *If you can act like you are rich, you can feel like you are rich, and if you can feel like you are rich, you can be rich.* If you can act like you are healthy, you can feel like you are healthy, and if you can feel like you are healthy, you can be healthy. All of these laws are fundamental and incorporate all secondary laws, such as nutrition, such as cleanliness, such as exercise. Any secondary law, that any school of thought recommends, is subsidiary to these laws about which I am speaking at this time.

Now, how do you get a feeling? You get a feeling by going through the physical exercises that you would go through if you were already the type of person you want to be. It is the number two portion of the "If You Can Count To Four" Formula.

The number two portion is, "*Pretend that you already are the person you want to be.*"

Pretend that you already have what you want to have. That is the appropriating of the law of reversibility. I did not go into this law in the original discussion on the *If You Can Count To Four Formula* because I wanted to keep it very, very simple indeed.

However, through starting with action, if you will start with action, you can create the feeling, the type of action that you would be in engaged in if you were the person that you want to

If You Can Count to Four - 119

be and if you already had the things that you want to have. Go through that action and go through it over and over again until you feel very strongly about it, Then as soon as you feel strongly about it, it must become experience. There is no way to stop it other than neutralizing it by giving your subconscious a counter demand or a counter feeling.

Isn't it a wonderful idea to be able to know that you can be anything you want to be and have anything you want to have merely by going through an act? One of the greatest psychologists in the world (William James) said. "Act enthusiastic and you will be enthusiastic. Act like you are healthy and you will become healthy. Act like you are prosperous and you will become prosperous."

Those statements are based upon the deeper laws of the universe which are real and tangible and basic, just like any other law. So, with childlike faith, I challenge each of you to act like you are the person you want to be, act like you have the things that you want to have. Select that beautiful mansion in which you would want to live and think like it is yours and act like it is yours. Go through the action of going out to it as though it were yours. Pick out that lovely automobile and act like it is yours. Go through every moment as though it is yours until you have the feeling it is yours, and as soon as the subconscious is deeply impressed with the feeling that it is yours, it will go through all the natural means of obtaining it for you, even to raising the money. Yes, this covers the financial as well as all other aspects.

So, this law of reversibility is the law that we must learn to use in order to get the feeling.

Very briefly, I'm going to share with you this process, as I used it myself, in taking my trip around the world last year. Several months before we actually took the trip, we designed the idea in the coldest fashion. There was no feeling for it, but we began to act as though we were going to take the trip. We design our plans. Where we would go first, how much time we would spend in each place, on the absolute assumption that we're going to take a trip, and it was very interesting, indeed, to observe just how each time we had a conference, each time we acted as though we actually taking the trip, how the feeling developed in Mrs. Jones and myself and our close associates who were working on the plan.

If You Can Count to Four - 120

In a few weeks time, after we had been going through this activity or the law of action, starting with the law of action, it wasn't long before we had a very strong feeling about the whole trip around the world. Of course, as many of you know, we actually took the trip.

It became an experience and the law says that if you start with action, start with physical activity, which is under the direct control of the conscious mind, you can go through these activities, even coldly and mechanically, and if you keep on going through these activities consciously and mechanically, you will stir a strong feeling in the subconscious.

That may repeat again and again, that any concept, any idea that is well-defined and is well impressed with feeling upon the subconscious, it must express as an experience area. It has no choice, it is a law the same as the law of gravity, mathematics, chemistry or electricity.

So, you can literally be anything you want to be and you can have anything that you want to have if you will first of all identify it:

>*(1) Define it then play the game*

>*(2) until it becomes a strong feeling in the conscious and then express this concept with strong feeling on the subconscious, and then it must become an experience in your life.*

So, I challenge you to test this out.

Try to prove me wrong, if you will. If you will prove it is correct, it is a "truth" then you can literally be anything you want to be and you can have anything you want to have.

So, dare to dream largely and "make no small plans for they have no magic to stir men's blood."

16 - The Power of the Law of Repetition

We have been talking a great deal about the various laws of the universe. One of these laws I would like to call the law of repetition. We now know that we have what we call the conscious function of the mind. Also we know that we have the subconscious function of the mind, and that all thought originates in the conscious phase of the mind.

That we design our concepts, in the form of ideas, and we clothe these ideas with our words. We express them by speaking our word, or writing our word. When the conscious mind arrives at a concept and defines it in the form of an idea, then it expresses it as a word. A group of words make a sentence making a more beautiful design and the concept, through a series of sentences, until the idea is well-defined in definite size, color, texture and motive.

Through the conscious phase of the mind we speak our words, and express this idea over and over and over again. Each time we express our concept in a series of words, in a well-defined manner, this word or idea is planted in the subconscious phase of our mind, which is the female portion of the father, mother, son principle of life, and a little vibration is recorded in the subconscious the first time we express the concept.

The second time we express it, the recording is enhanced or a little more indelibly recorded. It could be likened unto sticking a needle onto a blank record and you, with your hand, fix this needle with a straight line onto the record and then you take the needle and run it down that same groove again, with just a little more pressure, until the groove becomes a little deeper and a little wider.

The third time that you run the needle on the same channel, it becomes a little deeper and a little wider, and the fourth time a little deeper and a little wider, and the fifth and sixth times a little deeper in a little wider, and so on, and if you were to run that needle up and down that group, say 50 times, it would be what we call deeply engrooved and a very definite track would be established in the record.

Well, each time we control our attention and express our word along a certain line, repeating over and over and over again and

If You Can Count to Four - 122

again and again a certain concept or a certain idea, we are making a track in the subconscious. We are building, what we call in practical psychology, a conditioned consciousness. We are building a habitual feeling, or a condition, from which we express a habitual feeling in the subconscious.

And it has been proved that when we go through this process, through repeating and repeating and repeating over and over again, a concept, that it will become established in the subconscious, as a condition from which we will react with feeling habitually, and then that is known as a part of us and as Solomon said," As a man thinketh so is he."

He is what he is. I am what I am and you are what you are because of the sum total of these conditions and the subconscious, which were established through the law of repetition, my first arriving at a concept in which we believe in the concept which we have a sincere desire to be established in the subconscious. We then establish it and that becomes a part of us, and is the sum total of what we are, fulfilling the statement that was made that as a man think it's in his heart so is he.

So, let us apply this from a practical point of view. Let's take an example of a man who at the present time is a poor man. He is poverty-stricken and does not express abundance. Then, if he is a poor man because of what he thinks in his heart, or the sum total of these conditioned concepts, which have been repeated consciously and unconsciously over and over again, then we have arrived at a principle.

We can find out how he became what he is. He is a poor man because he has a concept of poverty which he has consciously and unconsciously repeated over and over to his subconscious, until it has become a condition, or part of the sum total of all of the conditioned concepts which make up his entirety, so that he can say that I am what I am because of the sum total of all these conditions.

Now, in as much as that is true, then if he can get a concept of abundance and get it well-defined and his conscious mind, and then if he will give attention to this new concept over and over again, and write it out in words so that it means something definite to him in the form of an abundant concept of life, so that he can speak his word or write his word over and over, and over again, taking advantage of this tremendous law of

If You Can Count to Four - 123

repetition, which, by the way, is as tangible as electricity, gravity, mathematics and chemistry, then he can build it, this new condition in the subconscious in the form of an abundant condition.

And, when he does that, he neutralizes the old concept, or the old condition, based upon a poverty concept and, as soon as he has repeated and gives attention to this new abundant concept, until it becomes firmly established as a new and indelible, and the erasable Tract in the subconscious, he will become an individual. For he is an individual when he reaches the condition of expressing abundance habitually.

Now, through this law of repetition, we can deal with the area of cause, which is the father principle as was described in another chapter. A well-defined idea in the conscious mind is the father principle. A well-defined idea is planted in the subconscious, or the female portion of the mind, and then the son or the dream fulfilled is a result, or the offspring. So, we're getting down to basic causes when we are dealing with well-defined ideas and concepts, which we control through the imagination.

Through our burning desires we have that wonderful ability, that wonderful function in our minds, to design our own desire. We can put any design, any shape, any size, any color, any texture, and quality which we desire in our original concept.

We can work on it like an artist until we perfect it. We can add to it and take from it until we are satisfied with our design and its content, in the form of a well-defined idea. That is the first step. Then we concentrate on that, we think about it, we have a movement of thought in the conscious phase of our mind along these lines exactly, over and over and over again, until we establish this new track more strongly, more strongly than the old track of the opposite nature.

For example, we build the new track on abundance much more strongly and deeply than the old track which was based upon our belief in poverty. The same thing applies, of course, to the problem of happiness, harmony and peace of mind. The only reason the average person doesn't have happiness is because they have a conditioned concept, established through this long repetition, on the opposite of happiness, which is unhappiness and inharmony.

If You Can Count to Four - 124

They have learned to react, habitually, inharmoniously or negatively to life situations. Thousands and thousands of times they have reacted negatively to life situations until they have a negative consciousness in the subconscious from which they habitually react.

They can consciously decide, through the will power, through the imagination, and not only can they decide through the will power, but they can design a new concept of happiness and harmony and peace of mind through the imagination, through a burning desire, and through this great law of repetition, then can give all of their attention to the new concept of happiness, harmony and peace of mind, until they build this newly conditioned concept of happiness, harmony and peace of mind in the subconscious.

Then it, of course, neutralizes, replaces for erases the old concept, and then we will react positively to all of life situations instead of negatively.

But I want to emphasize the power of repetition. The average person today is bored the second or third time they hear something. As soon as they can pronounce the words and as soon as they have a surface understanding of the words, they say to themselves unconsciously, "Aw, I've heard that before," and they are bored with hearing it again and again and again. They pull down their inner mental curtain, withdraw their attention and pay no more attention to it. Now that is psychological suicide.

You can never build a condition in the subconscious from which he will react habitually until you take advantage of this law of repetition. If you are introduced to an idea, and it appears that the idea, if it should become a condition in your subconscious, would bring you either happiness, health or prosperity, in all three or even two of them, then glorify that idea, insist upon reading it or listening to it or speaking it hundreds of times.

I have made recordings in the last 10 years of all of the cardinal principles of the universe, and I have played these back to my subconscious, not 100, not 1000, but sometimes many thousands of times until my subconscious is conditioned completely through these wonderful truths of the universe.

I had to learn how to listen however. After I had heard some of these things two or three times I've never attempted to say to myself, "Well, I heard that before." By the way, I have faced every problem anyone else has faced along these lines. Things have not always come easy. I have gone through the "school of hard knocks." I've had to learn to enjoy repetition. That is one of the most wonderful things that I could recommend to you, learn to enjoy repetition.

Attend meetings, attend lectures, read books. If they have a message for you that you are interested in, that you would like to master, you can master anything that you want to master, if you will repeat it a sufficient number of times for your subconscious. We cannot ever become anything in particular, unless we learn this law of repetition. It is one of the greatest laws in the universe. It is a process of learning like memorizing a poem. You have to repeat it over and over and over, a sufficient number of times, until you have memorized it and until it is recorded on the subconscious.

You not only want to record knowledge on the subconscious, you want to record wisdom. After you have it so that you can memorize it, then keep on saying it until it has meaning. By repeating it and studying it, over and over, it has meaning, and when you get the meaning and then how to apply the meaning, that is wisdom.

So "make no small plans for they have no magic to stir men's blood."

17 - Some Usual and Unusual Examples of The Count to Four Technique

Unless you have experienced it, you do not know it for sure. If you have experienced it, you can share your experience and you can recognize your experience in other people's experiences.

There are two major motives for sharing an experience. One is to impress others. The other reason is to help others. I am in the business of helping others, so I will share some of my experiences with you, along with some observations of other people's experiences, which means something to me, because of the fact that I have experienced something similar.

Some of my experiences will have happened when I was quite young, when I was growing up on the farm in Tennessee, as a member of a large family of 14. Some will be after I left Tennessee, when I was 18 years of age, and lived in Phoenix, Arizona with my sister. Some, after I was married at the age of 20, in Phoenix, in 1937, up to the time I started the big experiment with big ideas and became well-known as a successful businessman, lecturer, television and radio personality, world traveler and writer.

There are two major periods in my life. One, the many years of poverty and a feeling of inferiority. Two, after I discovered the secret of genuine success so that I could use it consciously, and became, what the average man calls, rich and full of self-confidence.

First, I will share with you what I call an unusual example then I will share several usual examples.

A Multi-Million Dollar Business

In 1953, I reached a point in my research and the "The Count to Four Technique" that I decided to really give it the test. I had discovered that there are great laws or principles in the universe, which are invisible, but tangible and real, just like electricity, mathematics and chemistry. *One of these principles is that if anyone will find a great human need, in which he has absolute confidence, and find an especially designed answer to that need, in which he believes with all his being, then burn*

If You Can Count to Four - 127

all his bridges and dedicate his life to taking the answer to the need in quality and quantity, that he will experience a large measure of happiness, health and prosperity.

I have learned that principle was not limited by precedent and that the formula was based upon absolute laws in the universe. So, I decided to start from scratch, and use the formula to organize a company completely from the standpoint of the principle of genuine success and the formula. My focal point of attention would be entirely from the premise of the secret of genuine success, and not from the usual business point of view. In other words, our first interest would be "the customer's point of view," not making as much money as possible.

We would operate according to good, sound business methods, but our motives, that is our first motives, would be, "expressing the principle of genuine success," which is a habitual attitude of rendering a genuine service to people. That would be our first source of joy. I knew that there is a law of compensation in the universe that always pays a man in the coin of the realm, yes, in dollars and cents, exactly, according to the quality and quantity of service he renders.

So, I knew that if I developed the habit of thinking, first of all, in terms of SERVICE, I would not only experience more joy and a feeling of gratification, but, since I would naturally render more quality and quantity of service with that attitude, I would automatically earn and receive more money.

I would be paid, according to the service rendered, so if I specialized in service and rendered millions of units of it, then I would become a millionaire in spite of myself.

Sounds like a beautiful dream, doesn't it? Well, that is all it was in early 1953.

I had done pretty well up to that time in many ways, but I had never really made very much money. I started with the telephone company in 1937 at $15 per week, working up to $30 per week by 1941. Then went into the insurance business, and, along with my research in the field of the mental processes, I earned as high as $500 per month average, until I went into the Air Corps in 1943.

As a pilot instructor for the Air Corps, I earned as high as $500 per month. Then, in 1945, I was back in civilian life. From 1945 until 1948, I went to college in Los Angeles, lectured and sold insurance part-time. I made a living during those years, but little more. In 1948, I became a manager for a large life insurance company, and from then until 1951 I earned $10,000 per year and up to $20,000 at times, as I was on a commission. But all this time, I had not saved any money to speak of. So, in 1953, I started with no savings. I had three mortgages on my home, a lien on my car, a note at the bank, and I borrowed several thousand dollars from personal friends. With an absolute faith in the formula, I started my dream.

One, *I identified my dream.* My dream was to help hundreds of thousands of people in the nutritional field. I wanted a stable sales force in the entire 48 states, Canada, Alaska, Hawaii and eventually the entire world. I wanted all the necessary business structure to carry out such an operation. I knew it would take office buildings, a large staff of executives, accountants, attorneys, communication specialists, sales people by the tens of thousands, operating capital, etc. I had nothing but a house with three mortgages, and a million dollars worth of faith in the formula. It said, "Just identify your dream, don't ask the price or how you are going to get it." So, I identified my dream and that is all you have to do with the Phase One part of the formula.

Two, *I started to "pretend" that I already had my dream.* I organized a company and used my dining room table for a home office. I called it my private suite of offices and elected myself president. I did not actually have a business telephone, a business card, or anything that looked to the outsider like I had much of a dream. But in my mind, I was the president of the greatest idea that had ever been designed.

Yes, in every way possible, I pretended that my dream was already a reality. However, at the same time, I literally went out and made retail sales each day, and along with retail sales, I hired and trained sales people as I had the time. I earned enough money, the first month by doing that, to pay my expenses. But as frequently as I could, I kept my mind on my dream. One of the things you do in the Two portion of the formula is to occupy your dream as frequently as possible.

While I was actually doing the work of the janitor, the shipping clerk, the bookkeeper, the stenographer, the office boy, the office manager, the sales force, and the Vice-President and the President in those early days in 1953, as often as possible, I lived in my dream of being the President of a multi-million dollar organization, helping hundreds of thousands of people each month. Yes, the Two part is to pretend that you already are what you want to be. It did not cost anything to pretend that I was already in my dream.

Number Three *is saying, "No thank you" to every interference.* I received quite a lot of what the average man would call discouragement from the start. One of my most trusted associates became disloyal to the principle, became excited over the financial possibilities and tried to steal the whole thing. I said, "I have absolute confidence in the Principle and the formula, therefore, this man's activities will not hurt at all." It, of course, did not. He has disappeared into obscurity and the dream has progressed beyond our dreams.

At various times, close associates have become disloyal to the principle and more loyal to the idea of making a fortune, and have vanished into obscurity, but the dream continues to grow and fulfill itself. Yes, number Three is very important. When you practice it, there is absolutely nothing that can disturb your progress in realizing your dream. I knew that, and have not been disturbed at any time.

Now, **number Four**. How did dream start with so many apparent handicaps and attain such stature in just four years? That is Phase Four of the formula. As I said, I started out working from my dining room table with not much overhead. I went out every day and sold from 2 to 5 retail customers. Also, I arranged to have two meetings each week. If I remember correctly, they were on Monday evenings and Thursday evenings.

I had been lecturing, for several years, on the Napoleon Hill Philosophy of Achievement, so at my meetings each time I would do several things. I would give a lesson on the Success Philosophy, then I would tell my story from a recruiting point of view, then I would give some help and training to those who were already in the sales force. So, as we say, I killed three birds with one stone. For some reason, my meetings grew and grew from week to week.

Pretty soon, men and women of high caliber were attracted to the idea and were trained to conduct their own meetings. We celebrated our 60th day in business by going to a nice lunch at the lovely Statler Hotel in Los Angeles. We had over 60 stable associates doing well the first 60 days. By our first anniversary, we had objective of 1000 well-established producing associates. We reached our goal.

There is a difference in having 1000 contracts in your files and then having 1000 producing, happy, well integrated people as your associates.

After eight months, I moved from my dining room table to a small suite of offices. My overhead still was less than $200 per month, as far as operating the dream. We were primarily interested, from the beginning, in expressing the principle, and not just building a big business in the usual fashion, so we did not try to impress anybody with a big front. We never have and we never will. The dream continued to grow.

In the spring of 1955, when it was almost 2 years old, we ran our story in a national magazine. That did it. We had already drifted into several states, through the internal premise of expansion, but now, through the story in the national magazine, we received letters from every state in the United States and most every part of the Dominion of Canada.

In a few months, we were servicing a few in the entire 48 states, and soon in Canada. Early in 1955, we produced a color slide sound film, which help to communicate our wonderful story a great deal. Our number of units of service doubled in less than two months after we obtained the "point of sale" film. All the time, from the beginning, almost every penny was put back into the business so it would grow and grow and grow in its capacity to help people.

Because of the nature of the principle upon which the dream was founded, and from which it functions, by 1955, several extremely high caliber men and women came to join the dream. Through these men and women, many others of their type came, to become associated with the idea. Pretty soon, over 1000 people a month joined the team. Then 2000 per month, then three, then four, and now over 5000 per month are joining the idea.

From the beginning, everything happened according to all the natural laws of the universe and the laws of the land. No laws have been violated. It has not been necessary to borrow millions of dollars as some businesses find it necessary to do, to build a business the size of the present operation. The most I

If You Can Count to Four - 131

have ever borrowed was $10,000, and that was when it was a year old.

Now, the dream is fulfilled in a measure at least. It has over 40,000 associates and over 5000 joining it each month. It is operating in 48 states and Canada, Hawaii and Alaska. A survey trip has been made of Europe, Asia, Australia, New Zealand and Mexico. In the next few years, it will take its expression to those areas of the world.

Yes, The Count to Four Technique made it possible to start from scratch and build a multi-million dollar business.

Learning To Walk

It not only works, if you will use it, to build a multi-million dollar business, but every time a baby learns to walk, it uses it. Let's analyze it. The baby sees adults walking and decides it wants to walk too. It identifies a desire. That's Phase One. It assumes that it can walk and it tries to take a step. That's Phase Two. It tries it over and over and over.

Its parents and brothers and sisters and neighbors try to discourage it from trying it too soon, but it goes right ahead and keeps on trying and trying. It pays no attention to them. That is Phase Three. Every time it feels the urge to try to take another step, it takes it, and soon it is walking. That is Phase Four. Every time one feels the urge to do something that would take him closer to his dream, he should do it. I feel that you can see now how everyone uses the formula in reaching every desire.

Buying A Mansion

I call this one buying a mansion because I feel that everyone should think of their favorite home as a mansion. Don't think of it as a shack.

I had a really dynamic experience in 1947 buying my first home which to me was a mansion. I had never owned a home. I had no savings, with the exception of maybe $150 or so in a checking account. At that time, my budget was $200 per month. I made a little more than that, but I lived it up, going to school and traveling around, lecturing, and not making expenses. But I decided that I would test the formula out in regard to buying my favorite home. The formula says that you

If You Can Count to Four - 132

can have anything you want to have. I said, "If that is true, then I can pick out the home that I want and get it. If I don't get it, I will prove that it is just a theory, and won't really work in practical things like buying a nice home." At the time, due to my actual cash reserve and average income, I should not consider buying a home at all. If I should consider it, I should, according to the advice of my conservative acquaintances, and my banker, buy an inexpensive one with a real small down payment and a small monthly payment. But the formula said to identify your dream and don't ask the price in the number one phase.

I decided to really give it the test and go all out on absolute faith in the formula. If it should work, boy, would I have discovered something! In September 1947, I decided to start looking for my dream home. I went to the nicest part of town and just looked from the standpoint of "do I want it" not "can I afford it." Finally, and not over, I found one that just "sizzled" me. When I saw it, every cell in my being said, "That's for me." So, I started my 1, 2, 3, 4 process. I put my name on it according to the plan.

One that is, in my mind, I identified it as mine. I exercise my mental processes on the assumption that it was mine. Each day, after I finished my work, instead of going to my regular home, I would drive out to this mansion as though I already live there. I did that day after day. I asked myself a thousand times, "How would I really feel if I lived there and people knew that I owned the property?"

Occasionally, I would show it to a friend of mine and tell him that it was mine, and my handball partner told me I was crazy. He knew my size, financially, at the time, and the value of the property. I just grinned and said inside me, "No thank you, you just don't understand." I kept 100% of my attention on the assumption that it was mine, still not considering the fact that the price was the price of a mansion and I had a $200 per month budget. Now, number four. How did I actually purchase the house and move into it just a short time later? I will be happy to give you as much detail as I can remember.

Needless to say, I finally stopped and called on the owner. He agreed to sell it. I did not tell him that I was broke. I merely told him that I wanted the house very much and it would take me a little while to get my affairs in order so that I could put all

If You Can Count to Four - 133

the money in escrow. I gave him two dollars as a token of my interest, and I wrote a binding contract that he would not sell it to anyone for so many days. He was offered a cash prize in the meantime, but he could not sell it because I had a two dollar binding contract for the period of time. I wrote a check for $500 which the real estate man said he would hold in escrow and not cash, as I did not have it in the bank. That is how I put it in escrow.

During the 30 days or so it was in escrow, I had a million ideas on raising money for the down payment, and how I could raise my income so I could make the payments.

The payments, plus a gardener, plus taxes and insurance was more than I was making at the time, not counting the fact that it would cost that much more to furnish it. The point I want to make is, that when one goes through The Count to Four Technique something happens inside your mind that will never happen unless you dare to test the formula.

After I dared to go through the number one phase and the number two and three phases, with no doubt whatsoever for a period of time, something terrific happened in my mind. I began to have ideas come into my mind by the hundreds that had never come before. Ideas on how to raise money for the down payment, as well as how to earn and received more income.

The average man, just like I had been up to that time, is not keenly aware that he must get some good ideas some way, otherwise he is stuck where he is. The formula, if you will dare to test it, will put your mind through the paces and developed it so it will give you a million good ideas. I needed several thousands of dollars for the down payment. I got the idea of writing several of my friends and telling them that I had finally decided to buy myself a home and needed $1000 to complete the deal. Several responded.

While I was in the service, I had loaned a friend of mine about $1500 and had considered it a loss, but I contacted him and he came through to help me get the house. I still needed $4500 on the down payment. I was in the real estate office one afternoon talking about my problems and it was rather humorously suggested that all I needed was an angel to just walk in the door and let me have the money.

If You Can Count to Four - 134

Just at that very moment a very charming elderly lady walked into the reception room at the real estate office. She inquired if she could find out who was trying to buy the lovely home next door to her, which just happened to be the dream home I had in mind and was trying to buy. I was introduced to her and we became friends. A day or two later I called on this lady and told her my story and she and her husband helped me to the extent of taking a third mortgage on the house. They were retired bankers from Canada. But, I still needed $1500 more.

It was about time to close escrow, and meantime, the owner of the property had become personally interested in helping me obtain the house. So, of all things, I had two cars paid for. One was a pretty good old "buggy" and the other one a second car.

My better car was worth about $2000 at the time, so I suggested that he take my better car for the difference. He did and gave me his old jalopy to boot. So the house cleared escrow and it was mine. It was mine, provided I could make the big payments. I started working on this project in September 1947. My wife's birthday is November 19th. I delivered a deed, that is a copy of the deed, to her on her birthday as a complete surprise to her. She did not know that I was working on the plan at all at the time.

Meantime, my subconscious mind had been doing some thinking about how to increase my income. I had been an agent for an insurance company since 1941. But now, I had to really get busy and do something that would double my income. I got the idea of looking around and applying for a sales manager's job with some insurance company. I made contact and became manager of a large life insurance company for the county in which was located my new dream home. I went to work day and night selling insurance, hiring and training men to sell life insurance and believe it or not, I made the payments and lived in the dream home from January 1948, until January 1955, until the 1,2,3,4 formula had worked so well, that I moved into my next dream home.

And, by the way, just last week I moved again to a nicer dream home still, where a 48 foot yacht sits in the private pier in the front yard. It is impossible to convey all the mental processes that take place in an experience like that. But I hope this experience will give many of you the courage to test the

If You Can Count to Four - 135

formula, as it has certainly worked in every case for me. I know now that it works.

Having Your Own Television Program

I have always been keenly interested in doing as much good for others as possible.

When television came along in the middle 40s, I immediately saw the vast possibilities of getting a message across to the millions on television. So, I said to myself that one day I would have my own program.

I wanted to share my message to others, via television, very much. In 1954, I decided that the time had come to start the 1,2,3,4 process.

So, we started it and went through the entire process. I identified myself as a television personality and every time I stood before an audience, I imagined that I was on television. I went through the 1,2,3, phases for a year, and part of phase 4. I did everything that I felt the urge to do. I went down to the various television stations and talk to them and told them of my ideas. I received nothing but discouragement for the first year.

One day, a man called me on the telephone. He said, "I hear that you are planning on doing a program on television, I think that I can help you." At first, I said, "No, I am working with several other ideas right now." But he insisted on arranging to have lunch with me. I had lunch with Ralph Rogers, and during our lunch together, I felt that at last I had found a man who understood my feelings, my true desire to do something for humanity. We began our work together in April 1955. In June, I started my first television program. I did 26 weeks on the ABC outlet in Los Angeles in 1955.

In 1956, I did 13 weeks on the ABC outlet in Minneapolis, Minnesota and Nashville, Tennessee. Also, under Ralph Rogers direction, I did 65 radio programs in 1956. I wrote 13 little booklets on the secrets of success in 1955 and have sold over 500,000 copies. At this time, we are filming shows for a syndicated network television program this fall. The 1,2,3,4 formula has worked again.

Writing a Book

For many years, I have had the idea that someday I would like to record my concept of success in a full-length book. But I did not want to just write a book. I wanted the finest title, the finest material that could be written from the standpoint of helping the average man. In the middle of 1956, I decided to test the formula, which at that time, I called the Alpha and the Omega. I did not call it The Count to Four Technique then. But the principal and the process was exactly the same. Anyway, I decided to identify the idea of the perfect title for my new book, which I would write as soon as I got the perfect title. I went through the whole process, over and over and over again. In fact, while on the trip around the world from October 15 to January 1, I did a lot of pretending that I had a real great title for my new book. 100 or more titles came through, but each time, my wife and I agreed that none of them were the real one. We knew, that when it did come, we would just know that it was the exact right one. No doubt about it!

Well, on January 24, 1957, I was in Cincinnati, Ohio, lecturing in a series. While taking a little nap, just before dinner at the hotel, I was half asleep and half awake, and my subconscious was really in a tizzy. It came through, just like a neon sign across the sky. "If You Can Count to Four. You can be anything you want to be and have anything you want to have".

I knew that was it. I told my wife about it and she agreed, indeed, that was it. We called our Sales Manager, Mr. Earl Shoaff, and his wife, in the suite next to us, and told them about it, and they agreed right away that that was "it." We called the home office, and arranged a conference telephone set up with our executive staff and told them about it, and they all agreed that, at last, it had come through. So, the book is now written and you are reading "If You Can Count to Four" because of the principle behind the formula itself.

A Hayseed Moves To Town

As I have said, I was raised in a rural section of the middle part of the state of Tennessee in a large family of 14. We were poor, as far as this world's goods were concerned, but my parents were the finest in the world. They had a large measure of the great values of the universe, which I call integrity, faith, courage and humility. I wore patched overalls to high school. I

If You Can Count to Four - 137

wanted to go to school more than anything else, and even though I had neither good clothes, nor any books, not even a pen or pencil of my own. The state did not furnish those things in those days.

I wanted an education so badly that I suffered the humiliation of wearing patched overalls to high school. This happened especially the first two years while I was attending a school called the Dibrell High School, a country high school about 6 or 7 miles from our farm. I rode a bus to this school.

In those days, there was a distinct caste system. The city boy and the country boy were so different that it appeared as though they were of different colors and lived in different countries. I was a poor, country boy. I do not think that any boy could ever feel anymore inadequate, inferior or more uncomfortable than I did. But I wanted to be a city boy more than anything in the world at that time.

I happened to be a pretty good basketball player during my freshman year and also my sophomore year. In 1934, while I was attending Dibrell High School, the county school, as a sophomore, the basketball team on which I was playing, won the district tournament. I made more points during the tournament than any player, even though I was playing the most unlikely position, which was called "back guard" at that time. I came to the special attention of the coach of the city high school because of my basketball efficiency. He invited me to come to the city in the fall and play football. I had never seen a football game at the time. The Dibrell High School did not have a football team and the city high school had had one for only a few years.

To my little mind at the time, to go to the city and attend school and play football was the most sizzling thing that could ever have been suggested to me. I was on fire for sure. My dear father was never athletically minded. He was too busy trying to make a little money so that his big, wonderful family could keep soul and body together.

I went home from the basketball tournament at all excited over the idea of going to town the next fall to school and play football. Boy! Did my father hit the roof! He sure did shut me up fast. The very idea was "ridiculous, impossible and silly, so if I even mentioned it again, I would do so at the risk of having my head knocked off," as one would say in those days. Of

If You Can Count to Four - 138

course, none of the 14 kids ever literally got their heads knocked off, but we were pretty well convinced at times that we just might, if we should ever seriously entertain the idea of really crossing our wonderful, Puritan father. He was tough, and I do mean tough. At least he had us all completely convinced that he was.

But somehow, I, without knowing it at the time, used "The Count to Four Formula" on him. You see, the formula works if you will just identify your desire, pretend that you already have it, do not listen to any suggestion to the contrary, and do everything that you feel the urge to do that will gradually take you to your dream. I did just that with all of my being. Looking back and recapturing my inner thought movements, I wanted to go to the city and be a city boy, and play football more than anything in the world at the time. I was literally seething with a burning desire. If it had not been for the burning desire in my heart, I would not have dared go against my father's orders. I not only respected my father, but I was afraid of him.

One, I sure did identify my dream. I pretended all summer, as I worked on the farm, that I was living with my big brother in the city and going to the city school as a city boy, playing football on the city team, boy, I lived that dream ten thousand times that summer. I would not listen to anyone if they said it could not be done. I was afraid to mention it very often to my father.

However, as my feelings grew into a condition of mind, I would mention it occasionally only as a possibility, to my father. At first, he would just sputter with objections.

Gradually, he broke down so that I could at least talk about it later on in the summer.

School was to start on a certain Monday morning in September. I had assumed that I was doing everything so realistically that I had persuaded my big brother and sister-in-law into letting me come and live with them and thereby fulfilling my dream. The stage was all set.

On Sunday afternoon, before the Monday morning that school was to start in the city, my big brother and his charming wife came out to visit us in the country. Everyone, with the possible exception of my father, knew what I intended to do. I was going to leave home and live with my brother at the risk of being disinherited by my father. I wanted to realize my dream so

If You Can Count to Four - 139

badly that I was willing to pay any price for it. When my brother and family got ready to go home late Sunday afternoon, I was all packed and I slowly left the house and made my way to their car, and went home with them.

My father still would not tell me that I could go. He had been so conditioned all summer by my persistent expression of my desire, that he stood stunned that Sunday afternoon and watched the whole drama take place without muttering a word. I wondered just what he would do. None of us would have been surprised at anything. But he lived through it graciously. He had been conquered by the "Count to Four Formula" Which he did not understand at the time. He lived to the wonderful age of 78, and passed on to a new expression, and in his last days he looked on me with a degree of wonderment that seemed to say in his heart, "What power did he use?"

I went to the city school, and became a football player. I doubt if I ever became a city boy in the sense that they were considered in those days. I learned to live as one of them, but as it has been said, "You can take the boy out of the country, but you can't take the country out of the boy."

Trip Around The World

I told you in the chapter on "imagination" how the Count to Four Formula worked in regard to obtaining your favorite automobile. So I won't repeat the story, rather, I will tell you about how the formula worked in making it possible to take a trip around the world.

You know that there is really no such thing as "big" and "little" in a substantive sense.

Everything is big or little according to how it compares with something else.

Last year about this time, June 1956, I started planning to think largely. What would be the biggest test for the "Count to Four Formula" that I could think of? Here I was, dedicated to filling a great human need in the nutritional field and the success field. How could I express the formula in the largest possible fashion, to my mind in regard to my basic objectives?

I gave considerable thought to the idea. Soon, the idea of "taking a first-class trip around the world," doing research in

If You Can Count to Four - 140

the field of nutrition, economic conditions, psychological conditions, etc., was forming in my mind. Also, we had bona fide inquiries from several countries in Europe and Asia regarding distribution of our products.

I brought up the subject to a few of my closest associates at a breakfast one Saturday morning in a hotel in San Diego, California, after having given a lecture there the Friday evening before. We all agreed that it would be one of the biggest examples of the application of the formula of success that we could consider at the time.

We all started putting it through the "process." We define the idea. We began to assume or pretend or play as if we had already done it. (Of course, the fact that my associates gave me a beautiful globe for my birthday the year before had absolutely nothing to do with it). I had only gone around the world about 1000 times in my imagination during the time since I had received the lovely globe. Well, it worked like a charm. We breezed through the "Count to Four Formula" and the trip was planned by specialists.

Every detail was worked out so that we flew first class all the way, stayed at the best places, were met at each airport by an English-speaking guide and chauffeur, and appointments were made in advance with government officials, and key business people in each country.

We not only take care of our research, business wise, but it was my privilege to visit Edinburgh in Scotland and walk on the same ground that the great Thomas Troward walked. I visited India and talked to some of the great teachers of the Far East. I visited Pakistan, Siam, Singapore, Australia, the Olympic Games, New Zealand, the Fiji Islands, and spent Christmas in Honolulu.

Someone may ask, what did you do with your young children? What did you do with your many business enterprises? Were you not gone for months? Well, remember the Count to Four Formula takes care of everything. Yes, everything. We arranged to leave our two children with professional people. Our son, age 13, was in a private boarding school during the week and with my brothers and sisters and friends on weekends. Our six-year-old daughter stayed with our good neighbors, where she lived most of the time while we were at home. Neither of the children seemed to suffer for the two months while we're were away

If You Can Count to Four - 141

from them. We joined them in two months in Honolulu for Christmas where we spent two weeks.

My main business enterprise almost doubled in "the number of units of service rendered in any one month" while we were gone. When you really go all out on the "Count to Four Formula" everything works out well for you. The trip around the world was made possible because of the formula because it appeared that there were a hundred reasons why it could not be done at the time.

I might share with you the biggest thing I learned from the world tour. I learned that people everywhere are just wonderful people. That every country is doing the best it can at this time, considering the hundreds of traditions with which they are bound. It will take decades and maybe centuries to break the bonds of false beliefs and traditions and limitations in some parts of the world. But, at heart, they are wonderful people everywhere.

We came back to the United States with a new realization that we are in a country made up of free-thinking people, and we are truly the land of unlimited opportunities.

We have one language, one money system and one supreme national government that is founded under God and is dedicated to expressing the spirit of Abraham Lincoln, that is of being "a government of the people, by the people and for the people." I believe that we will always be that kind of a country and that kind of a government, regardless of what the doubters may say.

18 - Questions and Answers

Question: *"Is it possible for everyone, not just a few, to be what they want to be and have what they want to have?"*

Answer: Yes, it is possible for everyone, not just a few, to be what they want to be and have what they want to have. Every person on earth has a conscious mind and a subconscious mind. Our mental processes operate on the premise of a system of rules or laws, just like electricity, chemistry and mathematics. When any person controls his mental processes, according to the Count to Four Formula, these laws are brought into operation and he will realize his desires. These laws do not work for one and not for another.

Some know more about how to work them than others, that is the only difference. It would be nice, theoretically, if every person could study all about how to operate these laws, so he would become an expert. The plan will work even for those who do not know about them and probably never will take the time and trouble to study them. It is not necessary to have a so-called formal education to obtain your desires. All you need is the faith of a child and the will to work the formula. Electricity will work for anyone, not just a few, so will the Count to Four Formula. The laws of mathematics will work for anyone, not just a few, so will the Count to Four Formula. The laws of chemistry will work for anyone, not just a few, so will the Count to Four Formula.

Question: *"Is it possible for just anyone to work the Count to Four Formula and become a millionaire?"*

Answer: I would like to answer the question by stating that each person is an especially designed individual. Each person is different from every other person on earth. We all know that each person has a different thumbprint, a different number of hairs on his head, a different shaped face, head, body, etc. also, we now know, after many years of psychological research, that each person has a different purpose, a different mental outlook, a different taste, a different mental center, from which one's desires spring. Different people want different things. Different people want to be different things in life. It has been reported that in the United States there are over 10,000 different vocations, or types of jobs or services to humanity. We all know that there is always some person who wants to do each job. In fact, we have a person who is a specialist in each job. For example, prior to 1945 or 1946, we had very few men and women who wanted to be or had become television experts in the repair line. As soon as we needed expert television repair people, tens of thousands of people became specialists in that field. That has always been true and will always be true.

So, you see that each person, by his very nature, expresses desires peculiar to his individuality. There will be as many different sizes and colors of desires as there are people. So, if Mr. A. is the type of person, who says deep down inside himself, "I just want a quiet little farm of about 68 acres in the hills of middle Tennessee." He worked the Count to Four Formula either knowingly or unknowingly and became just what he wanted to become.

Some people, by their very natures, express larger thoughts that other people. *The ultimate state of happiness of a person is the gauge by which he can measure whether he is expressing thoughts in relationship to his nature.* Every person wants happiness.

Happiness does not depend on how much one expresses as far as size and color are concerned. It does depend upon how much one expresses of what he is designed to express as an individual expressing his nature. In other words, if Mr. and Mrs. A. who are designed to express true happiness rendering a service that is worth $10,000 per year, are forced to try to express in a $25,000 category, you would be destroying their happiness. Using the same analogy, if a person who is designed to express at a $10,000 per year category is forced to express as a $4000 level, he would be forced to violate his natural expression. Now, this does not mean that a person is born to express in a certain category all his life and that he cannot grow into a larger scope of expression. We live in a certain "state" which is the sum total of all our thought habits. We can be happy and comfortable in our present "state" for a period of time, according to our individuality. As we progress, we become discontented with living in the same "state" and that state of discontent is a sign that we should design a new "state." By using the Count to Four Formula, we move into a new "state" and learn to express ourselves comfortably there. So, life is an infinite process of arriving, becoming discontented, and then designing new dreams and having the fun of expressing in the attainment of the new dreams. Then, we live in the new dreams until the

If You Can Count to Four - 144

feeling of discontent comes again, etc. Life is dynamic! Life is expression! Life is a game! Life is activity! Life is endless! Life is in the living!

If you find that you are the type of individual, who by your very nature, is always thinking of rendering a large quality and quantity of service to humanity, and you like to express largely, one day you will find that you are rendering one million units of service to humanity, and in spite of yourself, you will be a millionaire. How much money you make is based upon how much service you render. If you are happy rendering 2500 units of service per year, you are just as happy as the man who renders a million. Your degree of happiness depends on how much you are rendering proportionately to how much you should be rendering according to your individuality.

No, you cannot become a millionaire, just by saying that you want to become a millionaire. But, in a sincere desire which comes from the depths of your nature and the center of your individuality, you can realize by using the Count to Four Formula.

You should ask yourself, or your subconscious mind, what you really want to be, what you really want to have. Then, as the answers come from a sincere heart, write them down in your notebook. Change them as you feel they should be changed. Gradually, you will know what you really want to be and what you really want to have.

Question: *"How long does it take to be what you want to be instead of what you are now?"*

Answer: In order to be what you want to be instead of what you are now, "It will take whatever time is necessary for you to feel natural living in your dream fulfilled." I decided, in 1942, that I wanted to be a pilot instructor. I felt most unnatural in the cockpit of an airplane. In fact, I had been up for airplane rides with a friend of mine a few times previously and each time I was sick to my stomach for three or four days afterward. So, when I decided to become a pilot instructor, I became sick at the thought of flying. But, the question is "How long did it take me to become a pilot instructor?" I had a burning desire to become a pilot. I learned that normally it took two years to obtain the training necessary to become an instructor. But at the same time I was 1-A in the draft classification and could be "called" in 30 days or so. In fact, it was almost certain that I

If You Can Count to Four - 145

would be drafted in 90 days. I learned it would cost me several thousand dollars to take private instruction, and I had just $150 in the bank. Yet, I wanted with all of my being to overcome all those factors and become a pilot instructor.

I did not understand the Count to Four Formula at the time, but looking back on the experience, I now know that I used it without knowing it. In six months, not two years, I was a pilot instructor and to make it sound more ridiculous, I was instructing instructors in an "instructor refresher course" in flying.

Yes, I was 24 years of age, in the summer of 1942, which was the first year of World War II. I was 1-A in the draft! I had no money and the thought of flying made me sick.

My boss told me it was impossible, my friends told me it was impossible and my acquaintances told me it was impossible. But, in the face of all those seeming "impossibilities" I, with a simple, childlike faith, One, identified my desire of being a pilot instructor.

Two, I pretended that I was already an instructor. I pictured myself as an instructor. I saw myself along the flight lines at the airport. I felt that I knew all the other instructors and the flight director of the school. I lived in this area until I became comfortable in it, then I went out to the school where I would be instructing if I were an instructor and introduced myself to my boss. I told him of my plan and my whole story. At first, he did not understand and seemed to think that I was a fool. But, as I called on him from time to time, he began to respect me and to help me.

In exactly 3 months after I started my flight training, I called on him and he gave me a break and put me on as a student instructor. In three more months, I was a full-fledged instructor and teaching instructors. I was able to raise the money and overcome my air sicknesses and I received a letter from the draft board that they would not draft me for at least 90 days. So, my assumed boss in the number Two phase, became my real boss in 90 days. I was able to realize my "dream fulfilled" in six months instead of two years. So, if you have a "burning desire" and express it in an "all out" fashion, you can cut the time down a lot. The point is, "Do something about it" and you can accomplish wonders.

If You Can Count to Four - 146

Another factor in "timing" of accomplishing your "dream" is that each idea has a season. Just like each seed the farmer plants has a season. We know that it takes so much time from the time a crop of corn is planted for it to mature into the harvest. The same with wheat, oats, potatoes, etc. We know that it takes three weeks to hatch hen eggs and four weeks to hatch goose eggs, etc. It takes so long for a baby to be born, and so long for a baby colt to be born, etc.

Ideas or desires are similar. Each idea has a season. But the season of an idea or desire can be sped up by the heat of your desire. If you plant certain vegetables in your garden, it takes so long for them to be ready to eat. But, if you put them in what we call a "hot house" they grow to maturity much faster. You can put your desires through the "Hot House" treatment, if you wish.

There is another time factor also. That factor is the relationship of your desire to where you are now with respect to where you have to go to attain your desire. For example, suppose you are in the habit of paying $20 for a nice dress and you go shopping for a new dress. If you find what you want for $20, you buy it right on the spot. You do not have to argue with your subconscious because it is already accustomed to letting you pay $20 for a dress. But, suppose you saw a dress for $45, and you really felt a strong desire for the $45 dress. You might pass it up that day and go home to talk with your husband about it. You might go for several days or weeks or months and maybe even years without it because you could not bridge the gap. But, at various times, you would be thinking how you wish you could have that $45 dress. You look and picture how wonderful you would feel if you had it. You live in your dream as often as you can.

One day, you will walk into the store and you will buy the $45 dress. You will have the capacity to make the decision the day you buy it. The first time you saw it and wanted it, you could not buy it. Maybe you had enough money in the bank or someplace to buy it but you did not have the ability to comfortably make the decision until you went through a certain interval of time, during which you experienced certain mental processes, which I will call exercises. You developed the ability to feel natural buying $45 dresses.

If You Can Count to Four - 147

Generally speaking, the length of time it takes to become what you want to be depends on how far you have to grow and how strongly you feel about it. But regardless of how far you have to grow, and how weak you feel at the moment, if you are sincere in your desire, and will follow the Count to Four Formula, one day you will realize your dream. So, keep on keeping on, and then keep on some more and know at all times that the "dream fulfilled" is a sure thing.

Question: *"How long does it take to get what you want, once you have decided exactly what it is?"*

Answer: The answer to this question is the same as the answer to question 3. I just wanted to cover both phases of the idea, what you want to be and what you want to have. I told you of the fine lady who changed from a 1949 Nash 600 to a late model Cadillac in 5 1/2 weeks. Remember, I was coaching her personally at the time and it was possible for her to get pretty excited and to develop a burning desire, thereby cutting the time down considerably. On the other hand, I know several men and women who have attended my lectures over a period of two or three years, and they still don't have a late model Cadillac. They say they want one and they are working on it, but the heat of enthusiasm is so weak that it will give General Motors time to develop several new models before they will complete the process and get to where they have the "natural feeling," to the point when they can actually make the big step and purchase one and enjoy driving it.

Again, each individual has a certain capacity to turn on the heat and express a strong desire peculiar to their individuality. Anything that you can develop into any "burning desire," on a basis of sincerity, you can have sooner or later, according to how big it is in comparison to your present habit of life. Anything you are sure you really want, but now don't feel too strongly about, you can wait a while and slowly develop a strong desire for it or you can go through certain mental exercises and hurry up the process of feeling strongly. Call in several friends whom you trust completely and discuss your desires with them. Explain that you want so-and-so, but you wish they would help you develop a strong feeling about it. When you go through such a process, you are "masterminding" it. You can develop a strong feeling faster by masterminding it.

If You Can Count to Four - 148

The main point is to start where you are with what you have and do everything you are asked to do in the Count to Four Formula. You will realize your every desire at exactly the right time when it will be best for you at all concerned. There is a great big intelligence in the is the and this great big universe in which we live and this intelligence works through your subconscious mind and helps you to work all the laws in the universe, to bring about the fulfillment of your dreams at the right time for you and all concerned.

Question: *"What do you do when you don't really believe that the Count to Four Formula works, but you would like to try it on an honest basis?"*

Answer: The purpose of question 5 is to share with you a very important discovery. It is what I call the "Law of Assumption." Let's suppose that you come home late some night and you are very tired. It is cold outside and you have lost your house key. You are indeed very eager to get inside where it is warm and get to bed as you are tired.

Now, here are the factors I want to call to your attention. First of all, you have a burning desire and the second is that the usual, customary, tried and proven ways of obtaining or not available. You want very much to get in your own house, but the usual way of getting in, which is to use the key, is not available. What do you do? You begin to try to "think up" a new way of getting in, don't you? You improvise. You assume that you have a way and try it. If it doesn't work, you just assume another way and try it and you keep on assuming new ways, until you stumble onto a way that gets you into the house, to your warm bed. That certainly is a familiar experience to most of us, isn't it?

Now, let's consider the same situation from just a little different point of view. Let us assume that this time, you remember that you read a book about a fellow who was caught in the same situation and he used a certain little technique and got into his house quite simply. Let us assume that he took a hairpin and bent it in a certain way and pushed it in through the screen door on the back of the house and opened the screen door and then the regular door opened right up and he was in the house. What would you do? Why, you would ask your wife for a hairpin and you would bend it, just like the man in the book. You would do everything he did on the "assumption" that it

If You Can Count to Four - 149

would work. You would do this primarily because of your burning, strong, obsessional desire to get in out of the cold and get to bed. Yes, we all use the tremendous "law of assumption" every day of our lives, whether we realize it or not.

Now, the question, "what do you do when you don't really believe that the Count to Four Formula works, but you would like to test it on an honest basis?" Use the "law of assumption!" I have used the Count to Four Formula and it worked for me in many hundreds of cases.

Thousands of my students have had unusual experiences with it. You certainly want to be something in particular, and you certainly want to have several things which you do not have, so stir up a burning desire and follow these suggestions to the letter on the "assumption" that the Count to Four Formula will work. When it works for you, you will not only know that it works, that you will have become what you want to be a you will have what you want to have.

If it doesn't work, you haven't lost anything, but you have exposed yourself to the possibility of having it work. But, if you do not try it on the assumption that it will work for you, you have forever lost the possibility of finding out that it might have worked.

So, I urge you to try it out on the assumption that it will work for you. I know it will work.

Question: *"What do you suggest for someone interested in reading some material which goes into the ideas and principles behind the Count to Four Technique a little more thoroughly?"*

Answer: I hope you are vitally interested in this question. If you are, you surely have a great future. I have found that reading and studying in the field of research is a continuous joy, and I have found that if one should live a million years, he could always find interesting areas of further research in the field of our mental processes.

I would like to share with you, a suggestion, which is one of the most effective I know in helping you to really learn the basic principles of success. In the second division of this book there are 13 chapters. I want you to read the first chapter each night, just before you turn out the light, for seven nights. Then read the second chapter for seven nights, then the third, then the fourth, etc., until you have completed the 13 chapters over a period of 13 weeks. Then start right over again for 13 more weeks, etc., for 52 weeks.

Then, do it again for the second year and the third, continuously, until you are saturated with every principle of this success philosophy. This book, "The Count to Four Technique," is enough for everyone to study for years. The purpose of studying philosophy is not to entertain yourself but rather to further develop your awareness.

"Awareness is the key to attainment." The law of repetition is one of the greatest laws of learning. If one will read this book over and over and over and over again, year after year, he can be immeasurably happy, healthy and prosperous. What else do you want?

But for those who really want to read other books and do some more exploring in this wonderful field, may I suggest a few books which have meant much to me:

- Collier, *The Secret of the Ages.*
- Troward, *The Law and the Word.*
- Hill, *Think and Grow Rich.*
- Grafe, *Get Rich in Spite of Yourself.*
- Murphy, *The Miracle of Your Mind.*
- Neville, *Awakened Imagination.*
- Wattles, *The Science of Getting Rich.*

Question: *"What will be some of the noticeable things that will happen to me, if I completely accept the Count to Four Formula and get into the middle of becoming what I want to be and obtaining what I want to have?"*

Answer: If you will completely accept the Count to Four Formula and start wholeheartedly appropriating it in your life right away, the following are some of the things you will notice as activities and changes in your life.

The average person has certain habits of thought which are like railroad tracks. The train has to have a track to run on, so does a thought. Our habits are the tracks on which our thoughts run. Of course, we can think new thoughts and establish new tracks

If You Can Count to Four - 151

if we wish to put forth the effort, but the thoughts that most people think are old thoughts, which they have used for years and years to the point that the tracks are well established, and they think the thoughts without effort.

Because of this, they think these old thoughts constantly. Pretty soon, they develop these old tracks so deep and strong that they resist new ideas because it causes them to feel uncomfortable. We all like to feel comfortable. We resist anything which will cause us to feel uncomfortable.

So, when you go through the Count to Four Formula, you accept new goals for yourself and go through the process of building new tracks and sometimes upsetting some of the old tracks. This process is an uncomfortable one, unless we feel very strongly about our new goals. This process is easier to accept, when we know what is happening, and are keenly aware that it is just a short process and will soon reach a new stage of comfort and the newly established track.

For example, I played football back in my school days. I remember very well each year when we would go out for spring practice, for 4 or 5 days my leg muscles would become sore. This soreness became so severe that I seriously considered giving up football many times. But, the coach would kid me and tell me that in a few days, the soreness would be gone and I would feel fine. Yes, that is exactly what happened.

After a few days, I could run all afternoon playing football and my leg muscles would never complain for a moment.

Our mental processes are very much like our leg muscles. When we decide to establish new tracks upon which our thoughts habitually function, we experience emotional pain or discomfort, similar to the soreness in our leg muscles the first few days of football practice.

But we know that in a few days, the new tracks will have been established, and the old tracks neutralized or he erased, and our new found life in the new tracks will not only be comfortable, but vibrating with joy because we will have reached our new objectives. We experience peace of mind when we're able to live in the actual dream having already been fulfilled. All men are seeking this feeling but few have found it.

Yes, you will have not only new "feelings," new emotional experiences, new habit patterns, but you will have new poise, faith, joy, love and expression. You will live in that new dream home in that new location. You will drive that new car, wear that new dress or suit, take that trip, sing that song, make that speech, marry that man or woman, etc. Yes, you will literally begin to go through a process of becoming the person you have always secretly wanted to be and you will begin to obtain all the things you have secretly always wanted to have.

I discovered this formula a few years ago. At that time, I was afraid, felt inferior, unhappy, poor and ill. In just a few years, this formula has, and I say this with the deepest humility and gratitude, brought me the fulfillment of many of my dreams. I am now able to express life without fear. Because of this, I have enjoyed abundance in every area of living, including personal expression and a very satisfactory amount of material things.

I feel strongly that the purpose of material things is to help us express life, according to our nature, not to impress others. I not only appropriate this great formula in order to live abundantly, but I do everything I can to share it with others, as I believe with all of my being that everyone can live abundantly if they will follow the formula with simple childlike faith.

When you follow the Count to Four Formula, I say that there will gradually be a complete change in your life. Your habits of thought are the cause of everything you are, and now have.

You will change your habits of thought, therefore you will change into the person you want to be and you will have the things which will help you to express your new personality.

Question: *"Should I list all the things I want to be and work on all of them at once, or just pick out one or two things and focus on them?"*

Answer: First, you should list all the things you want to be next and all the things you want to have next. Do not be concerned (overly) about what you want to be or the things you want next year, five years from now or as a life's goal. After you list all the things you want to be and have next, then you will notice that you have a feeling for the one or the few that you want most.

Sometimes we say we vibrate more to this or that now, more than to something else. Some of the things can wait until you can give attention to them. But when it is right for you to feel strongly about something in particular, which you have on your

If You Can Count to Four - 153

list, you will give your attention to it and for the time being, that shuts out all other things. Of course, you might for example, have several irons in the fire and you find you can only give exclusive attention to one at a time.

However, with training, you can switch your attention from one to the other and not let any of them burn. You can list all the things that you want to be next, and have next, and then, if you feel like adding new items to the list, at any time, do so. You are the only person in the whole world, who knows when and what to add or take from your list. Do not depend on any other person to tell you about this matter. Your Creator gave you the power, the intelligence and the privilege to decide these things for yourself.

Accept this honor and exercise it. Change your mind as often as you wish and apologize to no one. You are an individual and you are therefore different. You should not compare yourself with others. Compare yourself only with your idea or goal or dream. You can decide what you want to be. If you have a feeling that you want to be a great singer, and you happen to be at a station in life were the mere mention of it to your friends or relatives would cause them to discourage you, do not let that disturb you in the least. Your background, your education, your friends, your financial position, has nothing to do with it.

The only thing that you need ask yourself is "Do I really want to be it, do it or have it?" That is the most important thing. If you are absolutely sure that you want it, that is sufficient. Every desire, or idea, has within it, the power, the knowledge, the wisdom, the substance and the ingredients necessary to fulfill it.

Remember that! I know it is true because I have tested it a thousand times. Things are not true because they are written in a book, they are written in a book because they are true.

Question: *"Should I list all the things I want to obtain or just one or two or three and focus on them?"*

Answer: The answer to this question is very much like the answer to question 8. List all the things that you really want to be and the things you want to have now. Then, work on all of them for which you feel a strong urge. Some of them you will want to do something about right now. Others, you will keep on list from months and sometimes years before you get around to

If You Can Count to Four - 154

doing something about them. Relax, and live one day at a time, but keep looking forward.

Question: "Whom, and how many others, should I tell of my objectives?"

Answer: The answer to this question depends on many factors. Generally speaking, you should tell only those who you feel would wish you well and who would not discourage you. This is based on the assumption that you have already decided that you want something strongly, and that no one can talk you out of it. If you are not sure that you know what you want, then possibly it would be well for someone to talk you completely out of it. When you decide that you want to be or have something strongly, then tell only those who you feel will help you to obtain your desire. They can help you maintain or increase your feelings or enthusiasm. They can help you to dream of ways and means of reaching your objectives.

We call that Masterminding. Do not tell your dreams to the world, for the world, generally, will try to discourage you.

Question: *"Should I have a certain time each day when I read and reread my list, and think about how would feel if I already had attained them?"*

Answer: Yes, you should have a certain time each day to read your list. The ideal time is just before you go to bed and upon awakening. A good plan is to take about 15 or more minutes, just before turning out the lights to review your notebook and create a mood of having already attained your desires, then go to sleep in that mood. You will sleep in that mood, and upon awakening in the morning, the mood will persist. Then, review your notebook again upon awakening.

During the day, at odd moments, consciously think about your dreams, too. In other words, occupy your dreams as often as possible, so you can learn to feel natural in your new dreams. When you feel completely natural in your new dreams, they are actually yours.

Question: *"What do I do when I list something in my notebook and then cool off and decide that I do not want it?"*

Answer: Remove it from the list. Do not feel hesitant or apologetic about this. Everyone does it and it is a process of finally arriving at a strong feeling about what we really want to

If You Can Count to Four - 155

be and have. Change the list as often as you wish. When the process has expressed its nature, there will be items on your list that no one could influence you to remove.

Question: *"Is it satisfactory to make my list, and at the time think it is complete, yet a few days or a few weeks later, decide that I should like to add to it?"*

Answer: Yes, add to your list as often as you identify something else which you feel you want to be or have, which will help you to express life more harmoniously with your individuality. There is an infinite, unlimited abundance in this universe. You can express it as largely as you sincerely desire. Background, environment, education need not limit you.

Question: *"Suppose I list a certain thing, and after a long time, it still has not come to pass. Should I assume that the Count to Four Formula is no good and forget the whole thing?"*

Answer: Of course you should not forget the whole thing. Every idea, or plan, has a season through which it passes before it becomes mature and bears fruit in the form of the physical expression of the idea or plan. There are factors which I would like to mention that have some bearing on how long it will take to realize your dream as a physical reality: The size of your dream.

The size of your thinking at the time you start on your dream. The frequency of occupancy of your dream.

In other words, the time depends on how big you are compared to your dreams and how strongly you feel about it and how much attention you give to it. All of these are under your control, so you can give it the "Hot House" treatment if you wish to hurry up the process.

So, when you continue to want something, never stop. The laws behind the Count to Four Formula are absolute and always work. If you have not realized your dreams, and you have had the dream for a long time, do not give it up, for I can assure you that the fault lies not in the formula but in your failing to adhere to it. The formula will not fail you. If you want your goals sooner than it appears to be coming, turn on the heat of your enthusiasm, give your attention to it and it will surely be yours.

If You Can Count to Four - 156

If you can convince yourself that you really want it, you can have it through this Count to Four Formula. It may take you years, but one day it will be yours if you never give up and you keep on keeping on, giving your attention to it on the "assumption" that it is yours.

By the way, some people say that they want something, and apparently work on it from time to time, but inwardly, they think from the feeling that it is impossible to really get it.

In that case, it is impossible. As long as your inner feeling is on one premise and your word is on another, you're feeling wins. So, be sure that your secret inner feeling is on the same belief as your outer word.

Question: *"Should I compare my dreams with other people's dreams?"*

Answer: In a general sense, do not compare your dreams with the dreams of others.

Do not compare them in a competitive way. You are different and especially designed.

You are an individual. You are designed to be and do special things. There is no other person in the world just like you and designed to do exactly the things you are supposed to do. So dare to be yourself. Oh, yes, you can study the deeper character of other persons and emulate those, but not the outer or externals of that person. Trying to compare and compete with other people is the basis of all the feelings of inferiority and many of the complexes people experience in their emotional realm. You are the standard as far as you are concerned. So choose your goal, the one you like.

Dare to be yourself!

Bonus – The Millionaire Maker Lecture:

"How To Get Everything You Want Out Of Life"

One of Dr. J. B. Jones most famous students – who himself went on to train Jim Rohn and others – was J. Earl Shoaff, also known as the Millionaire Maker.

Below is a rare transcript of one of the few recordings still existing out of his many inspirational speeches.

This is included here as further example of how to apply the Count to Four Technique in your own life.

- - - -

Transcript of a 1962 speech by J. Earl Shoaff given live from the Essex House in New York City.

I just want to take a few moments and cover some things that have assisted me in acquiring things in my life.

I know that few people are aware of these basic fundamental laws that operate in this world of ours. Some people are aware of them; some people are not aware of them, but they are using them. And sometimes we wonder why certain things happen to us, we acquire certain things and then over a period of time it seems like we live in stagnation. Nothing happens; nothing takes place; everything seems to be at a standstill.

There are basic laws in this universe that we are governed by and will work for you if you know how to apply them. And I would like to cover a couple of these laws that will assist you in knowing why these things happen.

For an example, everybody is aware of the law of gravitation. Now, we don't know how it works, but we know it works. It works for everybody. It doesn't matter whether you are a saint or whether you are the opposite of a saint. If you jumped off a 20-story building and you are a saint and you land on a concrete sidewalk, you are going to be an unhealthy saint. If you happen to be a crook and you do the same thing, the same thing happens to you. So basically, it doesn't matter if you are good or bad--if you use the law of gravity wrong you are going to suffer.

The law of electricity works for all of us. If we use it properly, we can light our homes by screwing a light bulb into a socket. If we stick our finger into it, then we get bit. You're going to get burned. We can burn your house down with electricity or you can light your home with it. You can cook with it. You can use refrigeration--all the great things that electricity will do for us!

You do not have to be an electrical-minded person. You don't have to be a genius to do it. A child three years old can push a button and turn the lights on. And one of the greatest electrical engineers in the world, all he can do when he pushes that button is that he can turn the lights on, too. So basically, it does not matter. It will work for you. We have laws to success.

We have laws of poverty. We have laws of lack, laws of prosperity. We have laws of hate. We have laws of love. We have laws of peace. All of these are basic laws. If we use them rightfully, wonderful things will happen to us. If we use them wrong, then we get ourselves in trouble.

Now, one of the things that has always bothered me, in all the books I've ever read on setting goals in life, positive thinking, positive goals in life--many of you have probably read some of the books--you follow these different steps, rules, laws, that if we set 10 goals we end up with 2. We lose out on 8. So it is not like the law of gravity seemingly, because it doesn't work every time. And one of the reasons it does not work every time, is that we do not use the right law. We are using part of the law, and so the law of averages will give you a percentage of your goals. That is all.

You say, "Gee, wasn't that great? It happened to me." But whatever happened to all the other goals you had in life?

I'm going to lay down a simple basic way and you can have anything material you want to have and you can be anything you want to be, and it's a simple basic situation. There's absolutely no problem to it. These are scientific things that work every time if you will do it in a simple way.

Now, the first thing we want to become aware of is we want to be like farmers. We are going to plant seeds, and these seeds that we plant are the seeds that we're going to reap. Now we're all aware that if we plant a seed of tomatoes, we are not going

If You Can Count to Four - 159

to get cucumbers--we're going to get tomatoes. If you plant a watermelon seed, you're not going to get grapefruit. You're not going to get radishes. If you want radishes, folks, you're going to have to plant radish seeds. And when you plant a seed in the earth, you must plant it properly. If you do not plant it properly, you will not have the harvest. One of the major problems in our country today for the average person is they take the time and the effort to buy all the harvesting equipment, but they do not understand the planting and the cultivating.

We want to reap harvest, but we do not want to take the time to plant, and we do not want to take the time to cultivate. Now the planting of the seeds in the earth is basically and absolutely the same process that you use in the mental world.

We are born with a conscious mind and a sub-conscious mind. We are the only animal in the kingdom that have both the conscious and the sub-conscious mind--a mind that can decide anytime in life where we want to go or what we want or what we don't want. We can decide with this accomplished mind of ours if we want to do a thing or if we don't want to do a thing. We can decide if we want to ear or if we don't want to eat. We can decide if we want a drink, or if we don't want a drink. We can decide what we want in life in a home, in an automobile, in the clothes we wear, anything that we want in this world--any type of furniture, any type of a home, any type of an anything.

We decide at anytime. Now, where most people are making mistakes is that they simply set their goals down. Now, what are your goals? Write them down. A fellow says, I want a house, a car, some furniture, I want some money. And this is the way they set their goals.

Now he has a whole group of seeds, let's say apple seeds. We had 50 different types of apple seeds, and we just grabbed any of those seeds and we throw them in the ground and they come up and they're green apples. I wanted red ones. That's because you picked any type of an apple seed. You didn't describe it. So we must learn to define.

Now, you've heard of the word "visualizing". You have to learn to visualize things. And when you visualize something, this is the thing that's going to come in your life, if the visualization is strong enough. Now we're always visualizing things in our life, but the tendency is to visualize negative situations. Now the

If You Can Count to Four - 160

reason that we're visualizing negative situations in our life is because, let's not kid ourselves, we're living in a negative world.

So if I say, "Joe, how are you feeling today?" And he says, "Good, fine." And I ask him the next day how he feels, and he says, "I feel terrible. I've got a pain in my stomach and I ache all over." And he goes into a...you'd think he was an actor. He can describe a negative situation in his body so wonderfully. But when he feels good, he just says, "Fine." How come people, when they feel fine, they don't say, "I feel great; I feel wonderful; I feel so great that I expect all the wonderful things in the world to happen to me today!"?

In other words, have a little feeling when you talk about the good things in life. I say, "How are you doing in business?" You say, "Fine." Now if he has a bad day, he says when I ask him about his day, "Lousy, let me tell you this is a...I'm just having a terrible time. Did you read that article the other day? It took me several hours to find it; it was on the back page down at the bottom in fine print, but I located it."

People love negative things. They seem to vibrate with them. For some strange reason, they don't want things that are negative in their life, but they keep insisting on talking about them. And they can paint the most beautiful picture of lost and lack.

I say by the way, "Internal..." and everybody immediately starts shaking..."combustion." A guy says, "You know what I thought you were going to say?" And he starts creating pictures and he says, by the way, I wonder about last year, what I did with that...I wonder if they'll find that...and immediately he says, I can see the guy coming in the door now...I wonder when he'll be here...I wonder what he'll look like... and he gets beautiful pictures, and the next thing you know, the guy is knocking on his door. He created the picture and he brought it into his life.

And the funny thing about creating things, folks: we are creators. Nothing comes to us. Everything comes through us from us. Everything in this world that happens to us comes from here, not out here.

And everything that you have in your life is exactly what you designed, the dress you're wearing, the coat you're wearing, the tie you're wearing, the necklace you're wearing, the home

If You Can Count to Four - 161

you're living in, the neighbors you've got, the friends you've got and the Senators you've got.

So don't blame me for people that you attracted! When you signed this person up, you're the guy that coached them in. You didn't care who it was as long as he came in. And pretty soon, you helped plenty of them and you say, "You know what, Shoaff? I've got a lousy bunch of distributors."

Well, when you understand these laws, you won't tell me these things. I'm not talking about you, or you--I wouldn't dare. There's too many here. What I am saying is that everything we attract is what we are, and what I am speaks so loudly I can't hear what you say. And what you are speaks so loudly I cannot hear what you say. So everything you say is the thing that you created. So be careful what you create. Be careful. It's hard to visualize a thing.

Let's try something, folks. Let's visualize a 707, shall we? What's a 707 look like? I've only been in one a couple of times. I've only seen one in the air once. It's hard to visualize one. You want to visualize an automobile, or a stole? I don't know why I keep saying "stole."

My wife must be visualizing a stole. I keep getting that feeling...every time we come to New York. You see, we have to learn how to describe things. Now I'm going to go through a description of a thing because this is very important in your life, folks. Please try to remember what I'm saying. You can change your life that quick. You can have everything wonderful in your life; you can have everything wonderful happening to you, if you use these few basic little things.

Now I'm going to describe a thing--an automobile. I'll talk about an automobile because an automobile is easy to describe, and people can comprehend it very quickly and very easily. I'm not going to talk about a Chevrolet; I'm going to talk about a Cadillac. Anytime I'm talking about a Cadillac, folks, I'm not describing the Cadillac per se; I'm talking about a Cadillac idea--the Cadillac idea in the clothing, in the home and the things you really desire deep within you. And I'm not talking about something that you say. "Well, I've got to have money to buy a Cadillac." I'm not talking about money. It's not necessary that you have money to have a Cadillac. There are many wonderful things that can happen to you. These things can

If You Can Count to Four - 162

come to you from many unusual sources. Many wonderful things can happen to you.

If you believe in the thing I'm talking about, your income can be doubled, tripled, quadrupled. The one thing that I had in my mind that I had defined in my mind was a red Cadillac convertible. I never had owned a Cadillac in my life. Now you probably don't want a red Cadillac. I wanted one, and I defined that thing right down to the socks, and the end result was I had me a red Cadillac convertible, and my income increased to a point where it cost me nothing. This is visualizing. This is a positive attitude toward the things you want.

Too many people stop their dreams because they start thinking about that thing that is not necessary in order to have it. I say to somebody, "Do you want a new Cadillac?" You say, "I want one, but I can't afford it." I say, "It has nothing to do with affording. I just want to know what you really want."

Most people are afraid to define what they want in life. They're afraid it's going to cost them something. Well if you're making $1,000 a month right now, and you double your income to $2,000 per month, you can have a Cadillac, you can have two Cadillacs, you can have five Cadillacs. Don't worry about the income-- I'm just talking about the principle now. The Cadillac--what do you do about it? I'll say, "Pete, what would you like to have?" He says, "A Cadillac." Now don't forget folks, I'm going to give it to him--I'm going to give it to him. He has nothing to worry about--no money, no nothing. I say, "Pete, what do you want?" He says, "A Cadillac." I say, "Fine, Pete."

Now this is where people make their mistakes. I say, "I've got a nice 1936 beat-up model downstairs. I'll give it to you." He says, "I don't want a 1936 model Cadillac." I said, "You just told me you wanted a Cadillac." He says, "I want a '62 Cadillac." I said, "Why didn't you tell me, Pete? Why didn't you tell me?" This is the way people set their dreams. He doesn't just want a Cadillac. Do you want an orange or a green one? He says, "I want a red one."

Now he's starting to define. And you know it's very difficult to define up here in your mind. The first thing you do is you get a piece of paper folks, and you start defining on a piece of paper. A 1962 Cadillac, a red Cadillac, a convertible--I'm just describing one car now. You can have any kind of car you want--a red Cadillac, 1962 convertible with a white top,

If You Can Count to Four - 163

red/white upholstery, a red floor, white wall tires, electric windows, a/c unit. The guy says, "How much does that cost?" I say, "Don't worry bout it--you're going to get it for nothing." The guy says, "I'll take it, then." Now he says, "I'm going to put everything down then." That's right--describe it right down to the tee.

And when he gets all through, the perfect visualization is up here now because he has described it. When you write it, you start seeing it. He gets the picture up here by writing it down here. This is how you define things that you want in this world. When he gets that Cadillac completely defined in his mind, he's got the seed. He hasn't planted it yet. He's got it picked out.

Now the important thing is that you must release that seed. You must release it and it must be planted. And the perfect thing in the world to plant that seed is to take this piece of paper now and write the concept, "Thank you". That's the law of acceptance. And you would be amazed how many people in this world can't accept their goods. You would be shocked. "Thank you" means you have accepted it. "I'm going to have it. I know it's mine." Then you take and you fold this piece of paper up with this goal on it, with this dream, with this desire and you put it away--put it underneath a tablecloth some place, put it in a drawer some place. Don't carry it around and don't take it out and look at it anymore. When you do this, that is planting it in the subconscious mind.

You've accepted--you've put it into the subconscious mind, and the thing starts to work. Now when you put this thing away, the reason you put it away after you have defined it: the seed has been planted in the subconscious mind. You put it away some place, never to be looked at again. The reason for it is like planting a seed in the earth, folks. If you go and dig that seed up two or three times a day to look at it, nothing's going to happen.

If you've never seen a lack of faith--it's the farmer who had the gullibility to dig up the seed to see if it was growing yet. Now that is little faith. He really believes in the laws of growth, and that's the same way with us human beings. This is the way we're making our mistakes. When we plant in the subconscious mind, and it's there, the dream is there. The dream starts working towards you, the Cadillac starts working towards you,

If You Can Count to Four - 164

and events start taking place out here, and the next thing you know it's getting closer and closer to you.

Now if you take it out, and you start to look at it, the thing that happens is we say, "I wonder where it's coming from." This is a true showing of a lack of faith. "I wonder when it's coming. I wonder how it's coming." And so you are putting doubt in your law, and it will not come, folks. It will not come to you.

Now, what's going to happen to the seed that you planted in the subconscious mind: you'll be driving down the street, you'll be in a restaurant talking to a friend and all of a sudden, there's a red Cadillac convertible with a white top and the whole thing will hit you again and you'll see your dream. And it'll keep coming back.

The reason it'll keep coming back to you is this is the only way that the universal law has of talking to you. There's no voice-- it's all in visualization. And when this dream comes up, what it really means is that's it's on its way to you. It is on its way to you--it's right around the corner. And so you do not at that time say, "How, when or where." All you do is say, "Thank you" because you know it's on its way. And then immediately put it back out of your mind.

And how would you act if you really and truly wanted a red Cadillac convertible--if you really and truly wanted one and it was a strong desire in your life, and you knew it was on its way, how would you act? You'd be excited, wouldn't you? You'd feel good--you'd say, "Man it's almost here, it's almost here." You'd walk taller, you'd look taller. You'd be happier. You'd be full of positive. You'd act different. Wonderful things are going to happen to you.

Where does the positive attitude come in at? It automatically creates a positive attitude because it's the law of expectancy. Good things are going to happen. You have planted your seeds properly, and they are working themselves to you, and you are automatically a positive person because all these wonderful things are going to happen. Don't just have one seed planted, folks--plant many seeds--any great desire you have in your life--a tangible object or intangible object. You can have anything in this world you want to have and you can be anything in this world you want to be by using this simple process.

If You Can Count to Four - 165

There is absolutely no way you can keep success from your door, if you will just follow this basic, simple little process that I just described. This is the law of life, and every one of you people have worked this process. Maybe you weren't completely aware of how you worked it.

But think about it--that's why you only get 3 out of 8 things, or 1 out of 8 or 1 out of 10, because you didn't know exactly the process you were using. Now you know the process, so you can deal with anything in this world. Children--our children, folks. How many times have you heard people say to their children when the child says, "I'm going to be President of The United States," and the father and mother will say to them, "You? With your studies, you'll never make it, Junior." Now this is a wonderful seed to plant in that fertile little brain. The subconscious is putting in the mind--telling him he can't; he's not smart enough.

The child says, "I'm going to be a rich man when I grow up. I'm going to have everything in this world." You say, "You? You're going to have to learn a lot, junior. You don't know how to handle money. You've got to learn how to use that ol' elbow grease." Anybody who's ever used much elbow grease, if he's ever made millions, I'll assure you the elbow grease is up here.

Now, what do you want to tell Junior? Anytime any children come to you or to their parents, you should tell your children, "Junior, you're the type of child who can have anything in this world. You have the ability and the intelligence to go anywhere, do anything and have everything in this world.

It is yours because you're that type of a child. Start planting these seeds in our children. This country today is teaching too many children, too many children, what to think instead of how to think.

And what are we? We are only children a little older than the other children. We are grown-up children, and we have to at some time in life, we have to start deciding and pinpointing things that we want in this world. And I'm not just talking about the tangible objects. I'm talking about intangible things.

What would you like to be? What type of person would you like to be? Would you like to have more love in your life? Well then, you must learn to give love. You'll never have anything without

If You Can Count to Four - 166

giving. Everything I have I receive back, multiplied. If I have a lot of hate in my life, I'm giving a lot of hate out.

And so if I don't want hate coming in my life, I shouldn't be giving it out. If I don't want people to talk about me, I shouldn't be talking about people. Everything that I send out, I get back with feeling. Every thought I think I don't get, because I didn't plant my seed properly--I did not have a true visualization.

How many of you ladies have thought of a beautiful dress or a beautiful something that you don't have. How many would love to have a mink stole? A few years ago, if my wife even mentioned a mink stole, the first thing that would come in my mind was, "Where are you going to get it from? How are you going to pay for it?" I did not understand these things. When you just say, "mink stole," do you know what?

I never was aware that there was so many mink stoles in this country--every kind of every price and color and designs and everything else, and if you don't even know the exact kind you want, how do you know if you can ever expect to have it? Do you know the amazing thing? The average person in this world, and I'm only saying this because we are the average people of the world, and I say average because I am talking to an intelligent group of people. I'm not talking to people way down the ladder. I'm talking to a group of intelligent people. And I'm saying this, and you analyze this yourself.

Ask yourself this basic question. Do you know what you want in life? If I were to ask you right now, "What do you really want? What is a tangible object that you want in this world--things you can feel and touch and smell?

What are the things you want in life?" And you know, folks, the amazing thing--I doubt if there's 2% of the people in this room who can tell me and describe it, and just like that come right out and say it. So, what is success in your life? What is it that you want? Define it. Write it down. Pinpoint every drop of that dream that you have in your mind. Define it so clearly on that piece of paper that you can completely see it in your mind. And when you get it written down, write "thank you" on it and plant that seed and put it away, and it will start to materialize and it will start coming into your life.

That is anything folks, anything.

If You Can Count to Four - 167

Now a guy says, "I'm going to put down The Statler Hotel." You know why it wouldn't work for him? I'm not saying it won't work for the fellow, but I am saying that it won't work for the average person. Do you know why? He couldn't even imagine getting it. He can write it down. He can define it, and he can put "thank you" on it, but he can never plant the seed.

And the reason he can't is because he couldn't even imagine getting The Statler Hotel, that's why. And don't forget, this is something you have to accept--you're going to have it, folks. I told people about a Cadillac, average people working on average jobs. I said, "Do you want a Cadillac?" The guys said, "No, no, I don't want no Cadillac." I said, "Well, why don't you want a Cadillac?" He said, "For one thing, it cost so much to operate them." You see, he doesn't want one--he isn't ready for that step yet.

Now see, he steps from one car to another to another. He raises his consciousness, until pretty soon, he can buy Cadillacs like the average person buys a pair of shoes. And you can grow; you can grow in your thinking. People say, "Boy, you got to be careful about people--they'll take you in if you're not careful." They get such a wonderful visualization--they're always getting taken in. So you see how we build these pictures in our mind? People will spend the morning; they're going to get ready for a wonderful day.

Tomorrow morning, we're getting ready for a wonderful day; we're going out and it's going to be the most exceptional day we've ever had in our entire lives. I said, "How are you going to start the morning? Exactly what are you going to do?" He says, "Well, the first thing I'm going to do is go out on the porch." He's going through his morning now--he's going to go out on his porch and get his newspaper and read a little bit about positive thinking in the headlines.

And if he can't find it there, he'll look and look and look and look until he finds something that is really good and negative and then he'll tell his wife and describe it, and he says, "Guess what I found in the paper?" And he starts telling her about some wonderful divorce that's taken place in the paper and the kids committed suicide, and he'll go on with this and he'll say, "Just imagine that, imagine that!"

And he'll describe it, and the negativity will get started and the wife will get negative and he will get more negative and when

If You Can Count to Four - 168

he gets all through with breakfast now, he's in such a nasty mood that he doesn't even like his dog! And he's going out to face the world with a positive attitude.

Do you see how ridiculous it is folks--some of the ridiculous things we do in life and we wonder why success doesn't always come to us in the proportion we'd like to have it come to us?

Expect wonderful things. Be a creator of ideas.

Let's not be moons, the reflector of ideas. Let's be suns, let's be the creator of the light; let's be the creator of the ideas, because we all have a capacity--that guardian of the gate, as the conscious mind. This guardian can at any time let any thought through to the subconscious mind it wants--any thought at any time.

We are thinking human beings. We have the capacity to think of anything, anything in this world we can think of, but we do not have the capacity to think of nothing. Now you try to imagine what nothing is. Try to get a thought of that--there is absolutely no way. So that means we are thinking human beings and there are thoughts flying through our mind continuously--a steady flow of thoughts all the time coming through the mind.

Now where do these thoughts come from? All of a sudden, you say, "Gee, that thought must have come out of the clear blue sky." You didn't think of it, and it might have been something you didn't even know about. And the thought comes through and you say, "Well, that's kind of ridiculous, isn't it? That couldn't happen to me." And so you throw that thought aside. And if it's a good thought, why not accept it? Stop and analyze it and accept it. And let them happen to you.

And these objects come through to you all the time. A negative thought comes through and you say, "Boy, that's a good and negative thought and you start thinking about it and pretty soon you get a frown on your face and you think about it a little bit more and you create a beautiful picture and all of a sudden you put that down in the subconscious and you think, "Boy, there's another bad thing that's going to happen to me."

Have you ever caught yourself thinking about something you didn't want to think about and you've been thinking about it for 5 minutes and all of a sudden you think, "What am I thinking

If You Can Count to Four - 169

about that nasty thing for?" We do it; we do it all the time, folks.

But we can stop now, any time we want, and we can change that thought and we can put in a good thought. If you don't want to think about oranges, change the thought and think about bananas, if you want. If you don't want to think about lack, change the thought and think about prosperity. If you don't want to think about hate, think about love.

If you don't want to think of anything negative, put a positive idea in your head. You know what happens, you can analyze and you can just dream about it and everything else, and get all these seeds planted properly and have all these wonderful things happen. Get twenty wonderful seeds planted, get them written down. Define. Thank you. Plant them into the subconscious mind.

Put it away, and every time it comes back into the subconscious mind and the law saying it's on its way, you just say "Thank you". Don't analyze it because it's already planted. Just say "Thank you" and go on.

Have ten, fifteen, twenty, thirty of these wonderful seeds planted and folks, you'll walk on air. You'll have miracles happen in your life. And don't be afraid to do this. Your wife isn't in harmony with the wonderful things you want to happen to you; well, if the husband isn't in harmony or if the children are not, or your friends aren't, you don't have to show them.

Plant your seeds privately then, and put them away privately and plant them deep and all these wonderful things will happen and you'll say, "You know, one thing about that person, I don't know what happened to him, but man oh man, everything they touch turns to gold. And that's the reason. That's the reason, folks--the proper planting of your seeds.

It was a real pleasure being here with you.

Thank you very much.

Supplement: Count to Four Technique Study Guide

Editor's Note:
From the key points Dr. Jones mentioned in this book, I've compiled a short set of excerpts to help the quick study and assimilation of his principles. These notes are presented by chapter.

Lessons: Introduction

There is an infinite abundance in this universe. Not only is there an infinite abundance of happiness, faith, love, courage, joy, humility, wisdom, generosity, peace, gentleness, meekness, patience, kindness, and all such qualities one could ever desire to express habitually, but *there is an infinite abundance of every material thing that one could ever desire to have in order to express his individuality.* So, the reason that so many people do not have the above in abundance is not because there is any shortage, it is simply because they are not aware of how to push the right button of appropriation. All things that one desires are available to one who understands the "Laws of Appropriation." In other words, there is a simple set of rules by which all things are obtained, which anyone who really wants to learn them can learn and then be whatever he wants to be and have whatever he wants to have.

If you will learn the ideas contained in this book and use it, I guarantee that you will realize your most cherished dreams.

Lesson 1 – The Count to Four Technique

To be genuinely successful, to me, is to enjoy a large measure of happiness, health and prosperity. It is a balanced type of life; Harmonious living with good physical health and also plenty of money.

So, it was my privilege to start out as a poor, unhappy person and to make the same observations that the millions are now making. It was my privilege to learn these basic rules and to take them out into the hard-boiled business world and to challenge every one of them. *And to discover, beyond any shadow of a doubt, that there not only is a system of rules, but*

If You Can Count to Four - 171

that anyone, not just a few, can learn them and use them and become just as successful as he wants to be.

The title of this book, "The Count to Four Technique" is designed to tell you that regardless of your background, your lack of education, your lack of knowing anyone who is supposed to be important, your lack of funds, or any other seeming lack, you can still be what you want to be and have what you want to have.

It has been said that 98 people out of every 100 have never decided just exactly what they want to be in life. That is, they have never come to any decision regarding a "life's goal" like Henry Ford, Thomas Edison or Andrew Carnegie.

Let's begin by looking at **Phase One** which is to i*dentify what you want.*

- Write it down.
- Define it.
- Describe it.

You see your thoughts as size and color and texture. One of the reasons a person is living a small, limited type of life now is that he is in the habit of thinking small, limited thoughts. So, for Phase One, *let's not ask the price.*

...[O]f the thousands of successful people whom I have studied, every one of them had either consciously or unconsciously developed the ability to think distinctly and clearly, and to define and identify the things which they wanted.

The millions of people who do not have the things they want, at the same time, have not developed their ability to think clearly.

Phase Two is also just a mental exercise, and it doesn't cost you one red penny. Phase Two is as follows: *"Pretend" that you already are what you want to be, and that you already have what you want to have.*

Ask yourself, "How would I feel if I were already the person I want to be? If I already had the things that I have written down on my Phase One list, how would I feel? What would I do? Where would I be right now?" In other words, assume the fulfilled dream.

Assume the feeling of the dream fulfilled.

If You Can Count to Four - 172

One of the best ways that I have ever used is as follows:

1. I first assume that I have already attained my desire.
2. Then I ask myself what event would normally take place after I had attained my desire but would never take place other than if I had attained my desire.
3. Then I make arrangements to live that event as though I had already attained my desire.

Phase Three is, *"That ability within you to say, Yes and No."*

Many people have not learned that it is their individual prerogative to evaluate any life situation or event or proposition and then down deep inside say, "Yes" if they believe it should be yes, and to say "No" if it should be no. I am not advising you whether, in certain circumstances, you should say "yes" or "no", but in order to emphasize this point, I would like to say that you have the power, and the right, and the ability, if you choose, to use it; and the God of Heaven gave you that power, right, and ability to use it.

Keep identifying your desires, and keep "living in the feeling of having already attained them." *Yes, you can control your attention units. You can learn to say "no" to anything which will hinder the fulfillment of your dreams.*

Phase Four is the *HOW!*

How do you get from here and now, to there, and what you want to be, and have what you want to have and not cost you anything?

Well, I am going to give you the answer in several ways so that you will be sure to trust it. First, let me say, that I am aware of certain facts, laws, rules, powers which are all natural, and which, if you will do certain things with the simple faith of a child, will all work for you and bring your dreams all fulfilled to you.

How many of you have ever had an idea come to you for "out of the blue?" All of you have, I am absolutely sure. Well, how many of you know just where the "blue" is located? I don't exactly know where it is located myself, but I know the name we give it.

The "blue" is your subconscious mind.

If You Can Count to Four - 173

Now, your subconscious mind is like the "soil" into which the farmer plants seeds.
- Well, Phase One is the seed.
- Phase Two is the watering, cultivating, sunshine and faith.
- Phase Three is keeping the weeds out and not letting the enemy destroy your seed which has been well planted and is being cultivated until the harvest.
- Phase Four is the Subconscious Mind, which has the same quality in the field of LIFE as the soil has for the farmer.

For example, suppose that you want to enjoy the standard of living which requires an income of one thousand dollars per month. But right now, your income is only three hundred seventy-five dollars per month.
- Phase One, you identify your desire of an income of one thousand dollars per month.
- Phase Two, you pretend and feel as you think you would feel if you already had an income of a thousand per month.
- Phase Three, you would insist on maintaining that feeling regardless of any suggestion which would disagree with you.
- Phase Four, you would listen for an idea from your subconscious mind which will help you to actually earn and receive the thousand per month. One day, you ask a friend of yours, "How many ways are there in the world, which pay at least a thousand per month income?"

The way to state the Phase Four principle is this:

The size and color of your thoughts are cause. Your experiences are effect.

Each thought has size and color or quality and quantity. Your thought regarding income is cause. Your income is effect.

If you could go through some sort of mental exercise and thereby increase the quality and quantity of your

If You Can Count to Four - 174

thought, which is cause, soon the income, which is effect, would be increased accordingly.

The Count to Four Technique is a mental exercise, which expands our thoughts regarding our desires and the law of cause and effect brings our desires to pass.

"If you can count to four", you can be anything you want to be and can have anything you want to have.

Lessson 2 - The Secret of Genuine Success

The answer is that any individual, on the face of this earth, can be genuinely happy, genuinely healthy and a genuinely prosperous if he will do just one thing.

Switch is focal point of attention from "How much can I get out of life?" and developed a habitual concern about, "How much can I give?"

In other words, *any individual on the face of the earth can be happy, healthy and prosperous if he will seek an opportunity to serve where there is an unlimited opportunity to serve humanity.*

The first compensation, to one who has dedicated himself to this secret of success of rendering a great service to humanity, is "livingness."

Of course, the great universal law of compensation proves to us that we are compensated, in the coin of the realm, according to the quality and the quantity of service rendered, and I would like to say that this law of success is not a theory.

The secret of genuine success is very simple. All you have to do is to find a great channel of service to humanity.

I would like to suggest, most strongly, that when each of you realize that *when you see limitations in your own individual lives and limitations in the lives of others, it is not because there is no adequate supply to fill your needs. It is because you are unable to understand the method of appropriating this infinite supply.*

List all of the things that you want to have, a beautiful home, a beautiful automobile, clothes and all of the things that you want to be, then read it over constantly. Change it as your

If You Can Count to Four - 175

desires change, and you will see marvelous changes happen almost immediately in your life.

I challenge you to learn the secret of success, to find a great channel of service to humanity, and then render it in a quality and quantity, and you can be anything you want to be, you can have anything you want to have.

Lesson 3 - Awareness Is Power!

...[T]he **first rule** *that I would like to share with you is this: We must become aware of the fact that we are thinking beings.*

Rule number two *is to be aware that you can only think one thought at a time.*

Rule number three *is that we must be keenly aware not only of the fact that we can think only one thought at a time but that we can control all of our thought processes.*

The only way we can establish this new habit pattern is through control of our thinking, the use of our will power. *Through will power, we clamp our new thoughts, our new concepts, our new objectives, our new desires, even though they are in conflict with the old habits, with the will power and hold them in place until we have the new habit established so strongly that it neutralizes the old habit.*

Rule number four: *I would like for you to realize, that what we are at this time, is the result of everything we have thought throughout our entire past.*

If I might quote the great Solomon of old, who said that, "As a man thinketh in his heart, so is he."

Note this. What Solomon said about a man being what he thinks in his heart is not true because Solomon said it. Solomon said it because it is true. It means something to us today, not because someone said it many years ago, but, because it is true.

Another great teacher of old said that, "Ye shall know the truth and the truth shall make you free." We know that we can seek the truth about ourselves and through the control of our thought processes, chart our future.

If You Can Count to Four - 176

Also, we should be keenly aware of the fact that whatever we want to be and whatever we want to have, we can be all of the wonderful things we want to be and we can have all of the wonderful things we want to have

- by realizing that we are thinking beings, that we can think only one thought at a time,
- that we can control this thought process by directing our will power towards that which we want to be until it becomes a habit,
- that we are what we are today because of all of the thoughts which we have thought throughout all of the past.

I challenge you to think largely and to make large plans, because they have magic to stir man's blood.

Lesson 4 - Choosing Your Goal

Our conscious mind has the ability of reason either "A" type or "B" type.

- "A" type means that we have the ability to investigate any matter, remark or situation before we will accept it as true.
- "B" type means that we have within us the ability to accept it as true on the assumption that it is true without having investigated it.

Now, due to the nature of the functions of the two major phases of the mind, *98% of the people do not understand the way the mind works*. They are the victims of every suggestion which comes their way.

In the "thought" realm, the idea concept is the father. The subconscious is the mother, and the result is the son.

..[I]t is my desire to make it quite clear, that *anyone, regardless of who he may be, regardless of his station in life at the present time, can discover his goal in life and by directing his attention to it, can obtain it and live a very happy, healthy and prosperous life.*

It has been said that 98 people out of every 100 do not have a goal or main purpose in life. That is not true. Every person has a goal or a major purpose in life. Every person was especially

If You Can Count to Four - 177

designed to serve or express life in some particular channel well. 98 have not discovered their channel as yet.

The Bible tells us to: *"Ask, and it shall be given unto us;" "Seek, and ye shall find;" "Knock, and it shall be opened unto you."*

If you have a quiet time, early during the day, you can use your will power to neutralize your negative mood, and dynamically outline a positive pattern, on the spot, for the rest of the day.

1. So, first of all, we define our goals.
2. Then we must develop a strong feeling, or a "white heat" desire for our objectives.
3. The subconscious responds to our desires to the degree of our feeling impressed upon it.

Many people do the following.

1. They assume that they already have attained their objective and then plan to dramatize an event which could only take place if they have already attained their goal.
2. Then, they play this little drama, and the subconscious is impressed, because it is implied that they have are ready reach their goal.

Your real and genuine desires will come forth and you will be one of the 2% instead of one of the 98% who do not know what they want to be or what they want to have.

Let me challenge you to know that we live in an inexhaustible abundance in this universe. *There is no limit to what you can be or have, except your ability to dream and believe in your dream.*

Lesson 5 - You Can Have Self-Confidence

I would like to introduce a wonderful word to you, which will mean a great deal to your happiness. The word is "consciousness." It means the sum total of all your beliefs.

Add up every thought or idea which you have ever accepted as true and that adds up to your state of beingness or consciousness.

If You Can Count to Four - 178

If you have accepted thoughts in the past which are not true, regarding who you are and what your relationship to other people is, then you have a consciousness of inferiority. You have that consciousness because you have accepted certain untrue things as though they were true.

Fill our minds with the thoughts of who you really are and how important you are.

- The purpose of life is to live.
- To live is to express.
- To express is to be what you want to be and to do what you want to do and to have what you want to have.
- There is an abundance of everything you could desire in the universe.
- There are laws or rules of making available all the things you desire.
- So all you need to do is to learn the laws and decide what you desire, and then do something about it.

It is your privilege to either say to yourself, "I don't believe all this" or to say. "I am open-minded and will assume that it is true until I prove it either true or untrue, inasmuch as it is good. If it proves untrue, fine, at least I exposed myself to the possibility of discovering that it was true. If it proves to be true, then I will always know how you feel happy, healthy and prosperous."

The first thing one must do is to be able to think it in the form of an idea. Then the idea is the seed, which falls into the soil, which is the subconscious mind. The subconscious mind then tells us, from day to day, what form of action is required in order to bring about the fulfillment of our dreams. We will receive this daily instruction in the form of urges and feelings. *Our part is to respond, with confidence, and do whatever we are led to do.*

Sometimes it takes years to realize our dream and sometimes it takes almost no time at all.

To gain self-confidence, may I suggest some things for you to do.

If You Can Count to Four - 179

- Read this chapter, each night, before going to sleep for 50 nights.
- Attend as many lectures as you can on positive thinking.
- Obtain a recording on self-confidence and play it over and over and over as often as possible to yourself.
- Cultivate friends who have self-confidence.
- Associate, as much as possible, with people who have lots of confidence.
- Expose yourself to every possible source of information regarding the study of your mental processes.

Lesson 6 - Money: What It Is, And How to Have Plenty of It

We have said that money is a symbol and is not the real thing. We have said that money is the medium of exchange of something real.

- Money also is an expression of the real thing.
- Money makes it possible for us to express ourselves in life.
- Money makes it possible for us to do the things that bring happiness.
- Money makes it possible for us to have the things which are desirable.
- Money also is a container.
- Money is a warehouse, or a storage unit, which makes it possible for us to render the real thing, that which money is the symbol of, in abundance.
- It makes it possible for us to render a service and money is a container into which we store units of service.

You can see how money is not the real thing, but a medium or a symbol of the real thing, which is service. In other words, *money is in effect, not a cause.*

Money isn't service, money is the symbol of service.

If You Can Count to Four - 180

We must be able to render a quality and quantity of service. Otherwise, we are not entitled to an abundance of the results of service.

The thing to do is to get a definitized concept of this basic premise. That the real thing in life is not money, but rendering a quality and a quantity of service to humanity, then habituate this concept by clamping it into place with our will power.

So may I suggest that you get a notebook and write down everything you want to be. You may think you want to be something that is going to take you years to accomplish. That is perfectly all right, write it down. You may want something that only takes a few days to accomplish, write it down.

Then, after you have written down everything that you want to be, on the other side, write down everything you want to have. List every category, your living quarters, your furnishings, your clothing, your transportation, the recreational facilities, like clubs, etc. several times each day, give some attention to this list, especially just before you turn out the light and go to sleep at night.

Now let us briefly review:

- Money is a symbol, not the real thing.

- Money is a medium of exchange, which is the great convenience in our modern society. By the way, we never should feel negatively toward money, money is good.

- Money is an expression, or, money is that which makes it possible for us to express the type of life which we want to express.

- Money makes it possible for us to enjoy life by providing a means of exchanging our services for the services of others. When we are in and accumulate enough money, which is the symbol of service rendered, we can enjoy all of the finer things we desire.

- Money is a container, a warehouse, a storage unit, through which we can render more service in any given space of time than we need for our own expression. We can accumulate this service in the form of money, which is a container into which we can pour this additional service and use it later date.

If You Can Count to Four - 181

- Money is an effect, not a cause, and so we do not put real value in money. We rather trust in our happiness and our security based upon our awareness of the real thing, which is cause, our ability to render a genuine, honest service to humanity.
- The great challenge is for us to learn how to render a real service to humanity. There are many unlimited opportunities to serve for every individual. Let us realize that we have been given, not only the privilege, but the capacity, to discover a great opportunity to serve humanity.
- Then let us burn all of our bridges and get into that particular channel for which we have been especially designed and let us become experts in that field so we can dedicate ourselves to rendering a quality and a quantity of service.
- We will be compensated in peace of mind and livingness, which is a continuous joy. That will be our first and most valuable compensation, but we will also be compensated in the form of financial remuneration in proportion to the quality and the quantity of the service we have rendered.

Lesson 7 - How To Make Success Automatic

Basically, success is founded upon the type of thoughts which we permit ourselves to entertain from moment to moment. These thoughts are controlled by habit pattern. *Once this pattern is established and our thoughts become an automatic process based upon these patterns which we have developed because of our own desires, it is possible for us to establish sufficient success patterns in the subconscious mind so that we automatically think the proper thoughts that will make us say the right thing, do the right thing and will make us automatically successful.*

This great law, which I would like to refer to as the law of *cosmic habit force* or the law of habit, creates the whole universe. Every phase of expression in the entire universe operates according to this law of habit. Every phase of intelligence in the universe operates on the premise of the law of cosmic habit force.

If You Can Count to Four - 182

This means that once a pattern is formed and is repeated enough time for it to become well established, it will automatically operate in that orbit of expression, unless it is consciously changed by a new decision upon it by the individual himself.

Let me review very briefly.

- Decide exactly what you want to be and decide exactly the things you want to have.
- Definitize them by writing them down and go over them hundreds of times in your thought processes.
- Think about the things you want to be, and the things you want to have, until habit patterns are established, in the subconscious, in the form of tracks upon which the thoughts can function.
- Then, when you feel natural in this new concept of what you want to be and what you want to have, it is yours.

Lesson 8 - How To Obtain The Missing Ingredients Necessary For Your Success

I have good news for all of these wonderful people who deserve to be successful, yet feel that there are ingredients missing from the picture which cause them to fail to reach their objectives.

There is a principle which makes it possible for them to obtain all of the missing ingredients, regardless of what they may be. I call this principle "The Mastermind Principle." *The mastermind principle is a friendly alliance of two or more people working together toward a common objective.* Employment of this principle makes it possible for a person to enjoy the benefits of the background, the education, the energy and the influence of other people as though all of these qualities were his very own.

This mastermind principle can be appropriated to help you solve any of your personal problems regardless of their nature.

Realize that there are experts in every field who will be happy to help you, provided you will ask them and then compensate them. You can compensate them either from the standpoint of your appreciation or from a standpoint of remuneration or

If You Can Count to Four - 183

something else that would be satisfactory and motivating to them.

Lesson 9 - The Power Which Makes All Desires Obtainable

There is only one power in the entire universe, but there are many applications and expressions of this one power. One of the most important expressions of this one power is what we ordinarily refer to as will power. Through the proper understanding of will power one can obtain the fulfillment of any desire whatsoever.

Let me emphasize this simple fact. Everyone has a will power. Everyone has a conscious mind. *Through the conscious and subconscious mind, we are able to design, according to our own specifications, the kind of life we want to live and the type of things we want to have.*

Through the will power, we direct it so it expresses itself in regard to our dreams until it becomes a habit pattern, so we automatically think in terms of our dreams fulfilled.

Lesson 10 - The Power of your Imagination

Through the proper use of the imagination, any person on the face of the earth can immediately assume that he is the person he would like to be. He can also assume that he has what he would like to have. But we must dare to imagine these things.

In other words, if you want to be truly successful, you must say constantly to yourself, "I am truly successful," not "I am going to be truly successful," because when you say you are going to be truly successful, you are confessing that you were not truly successful.

Then, the subconscious picks up the inference that you are not successful and brings that type of harvest into your life. But, dare to believe this principle and start saying to yourself that you are successful. *Say to yourself, "I am successful, I am happy, I am prosperous, I am poised, I am very healthy, I am a person of wisdom, I am a person of peace and happiness and joy and gentleness and faith and meekness, I am a person of enthusiasm and conviction."*

If You Can Count to Four - 184

Put everything you want to be in the form of the present and start making statements to yourself and the attitude of ability and prayer. That is the way the subconscious will receive it and will bring it to pass, in due season, when you do not lose your faith.

Lesson 11 - How To Obtain An Increase In Income

A few people in the world have developed the habit of rendering more service than what is expected of them. They appropriate the law of increasing returns. They sow generously, therefore, they reap generously.

Making the extra mile principle part of one's habitual expression for all humanity leads to the development of a positive attitude, and habitually rendering more service than that which is usually expected, tends to change our basic habit patterns from a negative to a positive and, of course, one of the most desirable traits in the world is a positive mental attitude.

In other words, it creates a continuous challenge to find new ways of rendering a service because it switches ones focal point of attention from the "I" consciousness to the "YOU" consciousness.

It develops the important factor of personal initiative, without which no one may obtain any position above mediocrity, without which no one may acquire economic freedom.

It develops definiteness of purpose, without which no one can hope for success.

One must render as much as he is being paid for in order to hold his job or to maintain his source of income, whatever it may be. One has the privilege of always rendering and over plus as a means of accumulating a reserve credit of goodwill, as a means of gaining higher pay and a better position. If no such over-plus is rendered, one has not a single argument in his favor by asking for a better position or increased pay.

Think this over for yourself and you will have the real answer to why it pays to render more service and better service than you are being paid for.

Actually, the employer is not the one who pays your salary, you are. You pay your own salary. It doesn't cost your employer a

If You Can Count to Four - 185

penny to pay your salary, provided he is paying you what you're worth.

So, the only honest way that any employee can ask for a raise is after he has gone the second mile in quality and quantity of service, to the point where he is literally earning and producing more than his present income would indicate.

Lesson 12 - The Power of your Emotions

The challenge is for each one of us to become aware of the power of our emotions, and the fact that we can control our emotions, that we can experience only the desirable type of feelings, and that when we impresses the subconscious with desirable feelings, we can have only desirable experiences.

All we have to do is define the type of situation we would like to experience and then began immediately to plant that kind of seed with feeling and emotion into our subconscious mind and make these impressions which will, according to the law as tangible as gravity, electricity or chemistry, develop into an experience.

If we desire to experience these desirable things as a matter of habit, we must entertain these thoughts until they become well-established and then the law of habit will come into play and, from that point on, we will experience them without any conscious effort.

Did you ever wonder why some sales people can say the same words, make the same approach, give the same presentation, give the same close, word for word, as another salesman and the prospect fails to react, while another person can come along and give that same approach, that same presentation, that same close and make many sales? *The difference is in the depth of emotion, feeling and conviction.*

It is a great challenge for each person to learn to feel strongly about something. Unless one makes a decision and says within himself, "This I believe, with all of my being" he cannot express life effectively. Each person not only must find something that is good, true and beautiful, but which expresses itself with the depth of conviction. Each person must take inventory of all of his present habit patterns and gradually as they come up and try to express himself to neutralize them if they are negative and replace them with a positive track or habit pattern.

If You Can Count to Four - 186

One day, all the negative patterns will be eliminated or neutralized and all of his being will come from habit patterns which are positive and manifested in terms of the good, the true and the beautiful. Then, every thought, which comes from one's being will come with sincerity and with a depth of feeling. This great indescribable emotional power will express itself effectively and one's life will become a beautiful thing, a happy thing, a desirable thing.

Lesson 13 - How To Get Started On Your Dream

All anyone has to do to enjoy a large measure of happiness, health and prosperity is to find a great human need, to find the answer to filling that need, burn all of his bridges behind him, and learn to take the answer to that need through a channel of service in quality and quantity.

...[O]ne must become aware that he is a thinking being.

Next, it is important that one become keenly aware that he can control the one thought which he thinks at a time through will power.

Next, it is important that he become keenly aware that he is, that everyone is what they are, because of the quality and the quantity of their past thoughts and experiences.

It is important for us to choose our objectives or our goals.

In order for one to be happy, healthy and prosperous, one must have an objective.

It is important that one develop self-confidence.

Everyone is especially and exclusively designed to do something well and possibly better than anyone else. Therefore, due to the fact that no two individuals are like or are designed for the same purpose, there is no intelligent basis for comparison of one individual with another.

- Realize that you are important.
- Realize that you are designed especially to do a great service to humanity and that you are different.
- Realize that you are exclusive.
- Realize that you have your own individuality.

If You Can Count to Four - 187

- Become keenly aware of your individuality, and your great purpose, and then dedicate yourself to fulfilling that great purpose, and you will develop self-confidence.

In order to get started on our dream, we need to know the proper concept of money, which is the medium of exchange used in our economic world today.

There is a great law in this universe, the law of habit.

There is a way for every individual to obtain the missing ingredients he needs in order to reach his dream or objective. I refer to the Mastermind Principle.

Consider, too, the will power, which every individual possesses.

Another very important factor in getting started on your dream and having the dream fulfilled is to become thoroughly acquainted with the marvelous imagination which every individual possesses.

The habit of going the second mile is one of the most important principles of success.

It is vitally important that one learn the power of the emotion or the power of feeling, because when the conscious mind uses the imagination, and definitizes an idea, that idea must be felt.

Another important factor in attaining health, happiness and success, is constantly having peace of mind.

First, take inventory of your present situation, relative to the size and quality of your thinking. May I suggest that you obtain a notebook and write down an inventory of your present situation, fourth dimensionally and third of dimensionally. You may wonder how to take inventory fourth dimensionally. Write down, in your notebook, your concept of how much poise, how much charm, how much kindness, how much love, how much faith, how much gentleness, how much patience, how many good qualities which are desirable, and how many bad qualities which are undesirable you possess as a matter of habitual experience at the present time.

That will be your fourth dimensional inventory.

Now, write down your third dimensional inventory. Your third dimensional inventory includes the type of house

If You Can Count to Four - 188

you live in, the type of car you drive, the type of clothes you wear, the type of income you habitually receive. Everything you have in your physical environment is in your third dimensional inventory.

Then, turn the page in your notebook and write down what you would like to be fourth dimensionally. How lovely you would like to be, how charming you would like to be, how much confidence, how much faith, how much patience, how much love, how much joy, how much peace, how much gentleness, how much kindness you would like to experience habitually.

Then, take inventory of the type of person you would like to be from the standpoint of the third dimension. What kind of house would you like to live in, what kind of a car would you really like to drive, what kind of clothes would you like to wear, what kind of a neighborhood would you like to live in, what kind of a country club would you like to join, what kind of friends would you like to socialize with, how much money would you like to have as a stable, basic income?

Number three, have a little talk with yourself. You are constantly carrying on a conversation with yourself, within yourself.

As soon as you learn to feel natural in your dream fulfilled, thinking from the position that you already are what you want to be and that you already have what you want to have, you will find that you have attained this new level of experience and you will be casually living in your dream fulfilled.

The way to get started on your dreams now, is to definitize them now. When you have attained the new level of your present dream fulfilled, you will be able to see further over the horizon of life and will be in a position to design a new dream of being and having.

Lesson 14 - The Four Greatest Values In Life

To me, there are four values in life which stand out above all others. They are as follows: **Integrity, Faith, Courage and Humility.**

...[I]ntegrity is a law, just like electricity, gravity, mathematics and chemistry. Integrity, when you thoroughly

If You Can Count to Four - 189

understand its nature, is something that one would not violate any more than one would violate the laws of electricity if one knew the consequences of such violation.

In order to protect the individual from the uncomfortable consequences of violating the basic law of integrity, it is necessary that we approach this matter of integrity from a standpoint of morality. In other words, we must lay down certain rules and we must say that it is good if we observe the rules, and it is evil to violate the rules.

Next to integrity, I believe that **faith** is the highest value in life.

In other words, our mind expresses through the instruments of our thoughts and our thoughts are contained in our words, which have size and color, design and texture. For when we say, "According to our faith it is done unto us," we are saying, "According to our inner perception and according to the size and color of our ideas relative to the infinite, it is done unto us." So faith is also a tangible law and not something that we just profess to blindly.

The next great value, to me, is **courage**. Courage is a function of mind that expresses itself in terms of intensity of attitude. Our ability to stand up and face life without fear. It really is a quality that is based upon our understanding, because our courage would depend upon our understanding, and according to our understanding, we will be able to react to life positively or with courage.

The next quality, to me, is the great quality of **humility**. Humility is that quality that comes from knowing who we are, in relationship to ourselves and our fellow man, and in relationship to the Creator of the universe and all of life.

Yes, humility is knowing the truth about our relationship to life, giving credit where credit is due. It is not the pollyanna-sissy type of attitude or the act that many people put on and call humility. It is a tenacious, stable type of thinking that comes from a habit pattern based on the understanding of life.

And so,

- **Integrity** is the greatest quality in the universe, and it is a scientific thing. To know the truth is to have integrity. When you understand integrity you would rather give someone $10 than to beat them out of a dollar. You know that the law will bring you happiness, health and abundance if you practice integrity.

- **Faith** is that size and color of one's convictions and inner understanding; and the amount and the quality that one is able to express proportionate to one's individuality.
- **Courage** is that quality which makes it possible for us to learn new things and face the things we fear in order that we might continue to grow in our understanding of life.
- **Humility** is understanding our true relationship to life, and not to feel that we can do anything of ourselves, but we can do all things through the great powers with which we are one.

Lesson 15 - How To Get A Feeling

It has been said by lettered men for centuries, and that to have a feeling of happiness is to be happy and have a feeling of abundance is to have an abundance, and to have a feeling of health is to be healthy.

Now, I would like to introduce what I call the *law of reversibility*, which is a law in this universe, the same as any other great law, like electricity. The law of reversibility could be illustrated as follows: if you start with a dynamo and a crank on a wheel, you can turn the crank and the wheel and turn the dynamo which we will refer to as physical action. We can start with physical action, and by using physical action, we can turn the dynamo physically and we can create electricity.

On the other hand, we can reverse the process. We can start with electricity, and with electricity, we can turn a wheel or a physical action. In other words, we can reverse the process, we can start with physical action to create electricity or we can start with electricity and create physical action. I'm sure that everybody can understand that.

Now, let's apply it in a higher level of values. *We can start with physical action and create a feeling and then in turn, feeling will create a physical action.*

If you can act like a king, if you can feel like a king, you can be a king. *If you can act like you are rich, you can feel like you are* rich, and if you can feel like you are rich, you can be rich. If you can act like you are healthy, you can feel like you are healthy, and if you can feel like you are healthy, you can be healthy.

Now, how do you get a feeling? You get a feeling by going through the physical exercises that you would go through if you were already the type of person you want to be. It is the number two portion of the "If You Can Count To Four" Formula.

The number two portion is, "*Pretend that you already are the person you want to be.*"

Pretend that you already have what you want to have.

So, you can literally be anything you want to be and you can have anything that you want to have if you will first of all identify it:

>*(1) Define it then play the game*

>*(2) until it becomes a strong feeling in the conscious and then express this concept with strong feeling on the subconscious, and then it must become an experience in your life.*

Lesson 16 - The Power of the Law of Repetition

...[E]ach time we control our attention and express our word along a certain line, repeating over and over and over again and again and again a certain concept or a certain idea, we are making a track in the subconscious. We are building, what we call in practical psychology, a conditioned consciousness. We are building a habitual feeling, or a condition, from which we express a habitual feeling in the subconscious.

And it has been proved that when we go through this process, through repeating and repeating and repeating over and over again, a concept, that it will become established in the subconscious, as a condition from which we will react with feeling habitually, and then that is known as a part of us and as Solomon said," As a man thinketh so is he."

Now, through this law of repetition, we can deal with the area of cause, which is the father principle as was described in another chapter. A well-defined idea in the conscious mind is the father principle. A well-defined idea is planted in the

If You Can Count to Four - 192

subconscious, or the female portion of the mind, and then the son or the dream fulfilled is a result, or the offspring. So, we're getting down to basic causes when we are dealing with well-defined ideas and concepts, which we control through the imagination.

You not only want to record knowledge on the subconscious, you want to record wisdom. After you have it so that you can memorize it, then keep on saying it until it has meaning. By repeating it and studying it, over and over, it has meaning, and when you get the meaning and then how to apply the meaning, that is wisdom.

(Chapter 17 and 18 as lessons are retained in full in this text – see these for study.)

Addendum

A collection of references, mostly long-forgotten and "lost", which will help you determine your path to the financial and life success you deserve.

- Robert Collier, The Secret of the Ages
- Thomas Troward, The Law and the Word
- Napoleon Hill, Think and Grow Rich
- Louis M. Grafe, Get Rich in Spite of Yourself
- Joseph Murphy, The Miracles of Your Mind
- Neville Goddard, Awakened Imagination – The Search
- Wallace Wattles, The Science of Getting Rich

- - - -

Also of Interest:
- N. H. Moos, How to Acquire a Million – Through Power of the Mind
- John McDonald, The Magic Story
- Henry Ford, My Life and Work

Look for these books as a series available from Midwest Journal Press

Resources

Visit Midwest Journal Press for more materials and related books.

http://onlinesecretsreview.onlinemillionaireplan.com/p/books-courses-and-material.html